Kids Without Horses

Other Books by Jennifer Spiegel

Fiction

The Freak Chronicles
Love Slave
And So We Die, Having First Slept

Nonfiction

Cancer, I'll Give You One Year

Kids Without Horses

Occasional Nonfiction from 2001 to 2024

By
JENNIFER SPIEGEL

RESOURCE *Publications* · Eugene, Oregon

KIDS WITHOUT HORSES
Occasional Nonfiction from 2001 to 2024

Copyright © 2025 Jennifer Spiegel. All rights reserved. Except for brief quotations in critical publications or reviews, no part of this book may be reproduced in any manner without prior written permission from the publisher. Write: Permissions, Wipf and Stock Publishers, 199 W. 8th Ave., Suite 3, Eugene, OR 97401.

Resource Publications
An Imprint of Wipf and Stock Publishers
199 W. 8th Ave., Suite 3
Eugene, OR 97401

www.wipfandstock.com

PAPERBACK ISBN: 979-8-3852-3153-9
HARDCOVER ISBN: 979-8-3852-3154-6
EBOOK ISBN: 979-8-3852-3155-3

VERSION NUMBER 010625

For Mom, Marilynn Spiegel.

The movie *Groundhog Day* was released in Germany with the title *Eternally Weeps the Groundhog.* That is so beautiful.

Theft by Finding: Diaries (1977–2002) by David Sedaris

"It's okay," I assured her. "I'm a writer."

A Year of Biblical Womanhood by Rachel Held Evans

"I would have been a good prisoner, had it not been for my need to speak."

A Place to Stand by Jimmy Santiago Baca

"The very idea that your private thoughts or feelings are worth sharing with anyone outside your family or friends is already a kind of arrogance. Arrogance is the exit and entry point to the humiliation that art requires."

Surrender by Bono

Contents

Acknowledgements | ix
Introduction | xi

I. Kids Without Horses | 1
   Kids Without Horses, 2022 | 2

II. John Krasinski Is a Superstar | 29
   John Krasinski Is a Superstar (2020–21) | 30

III. Love Rescue Me: Entering the Holy of Holies | 34
   This Will Be the Best U2 Essay You've Ever Read . . . and The Longest, Too (2001) | 35
   The Vag Soliloquy: A New York Love Story | 49
   Holy Ground (2020) | 56
   Nothing Sacred: Summer 2021 | 65
   An Untitled Poem | 74

IV. I Am Writing Blindly | 76
   Slaapstad: An Investigative Reporter at an International Rave at the End of the Century | 78
   Walter | 83
   My Defunct Political Book: Noah Baumbach's Mom Was My Landlord | 88
   Dear Rick Springfield | 115
   Not My First Time (2018) | 118
   Casa Padre | 122
   Meningioma | 128

V. An Ode to David Sedaris | 133
   An Ode to David Sedaris: When A Non-Famous Person Does What You Do (2017–23) | 135

VI. A Christian Creative Writing Aesthetic | 155
   A Christian Creative Writing Aesthetic | 156

Afterword: Marriage Scenes | 163

Appendix: The Moon Thought Thy World an Angel | 165

You Know That Song | 183

Big Thank You | 185

Acknowledgements

An earlier version of "Casa Padre" appeared on Roosevelt Community Church's blog on Feb. 20, 2020.

A much different version of "The Christian Creative Writing Aesthetic" was presented at the 2003 Conference on Christianity and Literature (Western Regional Conference): "Conflict & Reconciliation in Film and Literature" at Seattle University (April 25–26, 2003).

An earlier version of "Holy Ground" appeared in *Vol. 1 Brooklyn* on April 29, 2020. "Holy Ground" was happily reprinted in *The Furious Gazelle* on Feb. 21, 2022.

"Kids Without Horses" was originally a short fictional story that appeared in *The Gettysburg Review* (Vol. 19, No. 2, Summer 2006).

"Kids Without Horses" (2022, new nonfiction version) appeared in *Vol. 1 Brooklyn* on Nov. 9, 2022.

An earlier version of "Not My First Time" appeared on *The Quivering Pen* on Nov. 26, 2018.

An earlier version of "This Will Be the Best U2 Essay You've Ever Read … and the Longest, Too" appeared in *Image: A Journal of the Arts & Religion* (Number 31) in the summer of 2001. It was titled "Love Rescue Me: Entering the Holy of Holies."

An earlier version of "Walter" appeared in *you are here: the journal of creative geography* (Vol. 4, No. 1) in Summer 2002.

Multiple pieces were originally posts on one of my defunct blogs: "Bosco's Going Down" or "Okay, I Blog." I stopped blogging when I realized I could just go nuts on Facebook.

Certain names have been changed, but not all of them. Just a few.

Introduction

Listen. I'm not sure about this one.

This is my *third* attempt at an intro.

First, this was my Gen X book, and my intro would be about them. Sure, I'm obsessed by the probably arbitrary label, which, nonetheless, encapsulates my favorite things. Sure, I'm annoying my kids. *But I love talking about Gen X!*

My husband wrote a lovely piece on how ours is an epoch bookmarked by gunshots: John Lennon, Ronald Reagan, and the Pope on one end—and Kurt Cobain blowing out his brains on the other. I liked it; he made some strong observations. In between the gunshots, kids rode bikes without helmets, played Atari, got cable, made popcorn on the stovetop by moving around aluminum paddle-like pans, and expected to be obliterated by the Russians in a nuclear attack. A teacher went up in space in a space shuttle called *Challenger* and Gen X watched her explode. Between the bloody wounds of John Lennon and Kurt Cobain, Gen X blossomed.

Second, I wrote another intro, forsaking my husband's gunshot deliberations. I thought it best if I relinquish him from any responsibility for my wayward, seditious, Gen X swan songs. I just used my own words (so he couldn't sue me later). Herein, I promised in Effort #2, lies the *clash-bang-boom* of my era. Gen X is armed with wit and irony, and we will never fully have a good time at any party because we know that every party ends (badly), and even the drugs only last for so long. Gen X, self-aware, present on the scene but a little removed, too—looking in from the outside, no longer besotted by a space age, somehow still nostalgic for a Cold War.

Meh.

Third, this intro: This is my Covid book. #Truth.

This is my personal pet-project book. #Truth.

Introduction

This is my Book of Mourning. #NotTruth. That's really the book I'm working on next, tentatively called *Trauma Mom* (in which I deal with my children growing up).

This, though, is unorthodox orthodoxy. #Truth.

Unorthodox orthodoxy.

I like it.

This is a collection of miscellaneous, weird creative nonfiction pieces (not exactly aspiring to the status of "essays") meant to mark an era, *My Era*. It is myopic, personal, eclectic, and meant for *my* readers (miniscule but loyal, *so loyal*). I am grateful to the publishers, and that is #Truth.

Having recently dwelt within its pages to do some last-minute touch-ups, I'm struck by my own idiosyncrasy. I think there's a tremendous amount of dwelling on things going on in here. Like, I just can't get over my own cultural relics! I just can't move past my microscopic examination of what it means to be a writer. I just can't compartmentalize politics or religion or motherhood. But I can offer my readers *unorthodox orthodoxy*.

I can!

This third intro will stick.

Jennifer
Summer 2024

I

Kids Without Horses

"Kids Without Horses" was originally a short fictional story that appeared in The Gettysburg Review *in the summer of 2006. For years now, I've wanted to write the DEFINITIVE piece on my complicated relationship with my mother. (When I say "definitive," I mean "definitive for me.") That original story was actually pretty good, and I didn't include it in my first book—*The Freak Chronicles*—because, I think, I had other intentions, even then. I pictured a novel by the same title. The original was a barely fictionalized account of our 2003 trip to Ireland for my friends' fantastic destination wedding (Bob and Julie!). My dad had died in 2002, and we were venturing out for the first time. Later, I wanted to turn it into a novel, envisioning myself as some kind of David Sedaris/Elena Ferrante/Oversharing Writer-Maverick, tackling a difficult relationship. I tried a few times and failed. Problems persisted. The Biggest Problem: My Mom Is No Tim. My husband really lets me go wild in prose; I'll say whatever. Unmitigated pen. Sometimes, he rolls his eyes. Sometimes, he shrugs.*

Could I do that to my mother, though? Could she handle my unruly prose—uncensored?

My unorthodox orthodoxy?

The is the new "Kids Without Horses." It was written in 2022, and it's nonfiction.

Kids Without Horses, 2022

This is the timeline to know for this very long essay.

In June 1998, I suffer a brain stem injury when a tour bus rolls on a safari trip in South Africa. I've been living there for around four months, and I'm headed for Namibia. I'll never make it. I'm twenty-eight-years-old, and I will never be the same woman again. My mom is fifty-two (about my age as of this writing), and she literally has to fly from Phoenix to Cape Town to retrieve me, broken. My lifestyle is not so great. It's a profound disappointment to her (*I'm* a profound disappointment to her). I'll spend a big chunk of the end of June in a rehab hospital in Chicago, wheelchair-bound and very angry. My mom will be there. She'll spend hours with me in that hospital, walking me around and around the nurses' corridors, the entire floor—me, learning to walk again.

From June 1998 until August 1999, I live a new and unhappy life. There is rehab, physical therapy, speech and occupational therapy, figuring out how to pay for enormous medical bills, seeing miscellaneous psychiatrists that I don't give the time of day to, getting my driver's license again along with a spinner knob in my car, and applying for disability (I am rejected). My father sinks into a depression that he hides from me, and we will never discuss it. My mother plays endless board games with me that she supposes will help my coordination, and she doesn't reveal her fears or sorrows.

In the fall of 1999, I return to grad school to get an MFA in creative writing and start teaching college English. I got into the program before the Accident (*The* Accident), so ASU really couldn't turn me away. They give me the best writing chairperson to work with—probably as a charity act—so I am pretty much set. (He later ruined his life in a #MeToo scandal—but first he taught me to write.)

It's ironic and wild and a bad joke that I, brain-damaged, am teaching college kids. It's also ironic and wild and not a bad joke at all that my writing abilities are not only intact—but *better* than before. *I can freakin' write!*

Kids Without Horses

My first new friend post-Accident, Julie Hensley, tells me that I introduced myself to the other teaching assistants in some weird, awkward way. Both of us are middle-aged now and don't actually remember the details, but it was something like, "Hi. I'm Jennifer, and I have brain damage." Everyone squirmed uncomfortably. How does one react to *that*? (Julie is the one who later marries in Ireland—read further.)

In the summer of 2002, I am what I am. I work full-time, I drive, I write. *I can do this*, I guess I think. I'm about to put a down payment on a small house, because I've been living with my parents, and I'm still brutally unhappy. I fake normalcy well, but sometimes I mess up. Also, 9/11 happened, and the world is different. I'm thirty-two.

In July 2002, on a morning when I'm teaching Freshman English at a nearby community college, my dad is in a fatal car accident on Bell Road in North Phoenix. He had been driving home from the gym. Police say that he died "instantly." As the years go by, I wonder if they say that to everyone, as a kind of cold comfort. Do we really want to hear that it was a slow, agonizing death, and they tried to resuscitate him but failed? *We do not.* My mother, only fifty-six, meets me inside the front door, weeping. She clutches me in the hallway (I hear other people in the house) and she cries, "Please don't leave me."

So I don't.

I stay.

This is the crux of the whole story.

I do not leave.

I will resent this impossible mother-daughter moment for the rest of my life.

What if that had never been said?

In the summer of 2003, I finally move down the road (this does not constitute leaving), buying a small house that seems New England-y. (This is an ironic moment in my life, this faux-New England décor—for I will eventually marry a New Englander.) I teach college full-time. I get two cats and start living as a single career woman. It's a big joke, because I'm STILL feigning normalcy. I'm this big, huge fraud.

I never feel normal.

I can't hear out of one ear. I walk funny. I type with one hand. I physically don't cry, and I live with low-level constant depression. Sometimes, I say weird shit. Half of my body is what they call ataxic.

But I can write like a motherfucker.

Kids Without Horses

In the spring of 2004, I meet Tim. I think it's safe to say that we are both desperate.

In August 2004, Tim and I marry. I had not expected to ever get married.

From 2004 through 2012, my marriage is horrible. I cannot fully express the depths of my misery. Or Tim's, for that matter. It turns out, though, that I can totally have children—and we have two. Many, many lousy things happen. I know that during this time, besides the kids, a few things relevant to this story occur: *I make a very huge mistake of doing what every marriage book tells you not to do, which is to tell your mother how bad your marriage is; I publish two books; my mother has hip surgery—maybe more than one—and it is botched, rendering her unable to ever really be active again.*

Whenever this hip surgery is, I'm utterly not there for her. I couldn't even tell you when it was or what happened. In my own life, I wanted to kill myself, but I never would because I had two beautiful daughters, though every waking moment is unhappy, and I am confident that I will either die soon or destroy my children—or both. I see no end in sight. It is during this time that my mother has her botched hip surgery, which results—more or less—in her immobility for the rest of her life. I know, at one point, I sit in a rehab hospital room in Scottsdale with her in a bed and I'm on my laptop, and she accuses me of not being there for her, but just doing my own thing. Though I protest and deny it, it's true. *I just want to get away from life and sit in a rehab hospital while my mother suffers her devastating injury, and I want to be left alone.*

I want to be left alone.

What I don't know then is that, in the same way in which I'll forever resent her plea to not leave her, I'll forever feel guilty for not being there for her because I was too preoccupied by my own sorrows.

I will never apologize for this, because I am brain-damaged and not-the-same-person person I once was. I'll just live with that guilt.

I'll never be able to give the reader the chronology of the hip surgery or surgeries, and I don't even fully know what happened.

I was too sad.

She walked again but was not the same.

It was then that she became an Old Lady.

In 2013, in another story altogether, my marriage works out! It's not for this piece. All I can say is that I'm obviously not a good person, so I probably have very little to do with it.

In the spring of 2015, my family (husband and two kids) moves into my childhood home—the one I moved out of—and my mom builds an addition with its own door (which she humorously locks on us for the first few years) and she moves into it. She offers this arrangement, which really binds all of us financially and involves a lawyer, as something that'll "work out for all of us." With this arrangement—Tim and I and our children will be in the "main" house (where I grew up), and my mom will be in the addition—we'll get out of debt, and she'll downsize with her beloved grandchildren close by.

Secretly, she sees this as taking care of me and my kids in case my marriage implodes.

In the future, I will see this as an arrangement that she used to unintentionally trap me by making sure that she, an aging widow, is taken care of till she dies in some lay-your-head-down-to-rest death in which her grandkids surround her.

So, basically, she thinks she's taking care of me, and I think I'm taking care of her.

This is also how we'll shape our own narratives.

Her friends will see her as the caretaker, and my friends will see me as the stronghold. Her friends will see her as a mother *who loved too much.* My friends will see me as a wondrous daughter keeping her mom out of a wretched nursing home.

We craft our own stories.

In June 2015, I'm diagnosed with Stage 2 breast cancer, so all bets are off.

In November 2016, Donald J. Trump becomes president and I'm in remission and neither of us vote for him and my marriage is good. I'm no longer even bothering to feign normalcy. Who wants that? (My kids do!) My mom is aging, and I was there for it but not there, too, so I never adjust to that thing, that *distance,* that other people seem to have with their elderly parents. Even Tim has it with his mom: *separate identities.*

What does it mean to have a life all of one's own?

We never had that proper separation. But we are strangers, too. My life is now wrapped up in other people. I'm no longer sharing myself with her. I think she still tries to share herself with me.

But I'm gone.

Though we are living—basically—in the same house, my childhood home.

By November 2020, our relationship is miserable. Trump can be a symbol of our divide. When she supports him the second time around, I feel betrayed—and my hurt sticks with me, an open wound. I take it personally. When I reject her form of Christianity, she feels that I'm a heretic. My lack of her religiosity is rebellion, death, a downfall. There is literally *nothing* that either one of us can say that pleases the other. The pain is too much. We might only agree on pets and the decline of *The Walking Dead*.

In the summer of 2021, her hip is seriously infected. She is now elderly. I am now middle-aged and a mother, like other mothers are mothers. *I am Mom.* Tim and I made it. Tim wants to move to Massachusetts after the girls graduate high school.

Now, my mom and I are who we are.

This is where we are.

* * *

My mom is a lover *and* a fighter.

Formidable.

When my dad dies, she rises to the occasion. I literally cannot remember one instance of bitterness—not a hint. No *Why Me?* came out of her mouth.

She wept, and she got to her feet.

Too young to be elderly, too elderly to be young, Marilynn Spiegel got a classy job in a gallery in Old Town Scottsdale, selling upper-crusty art to rich people in the desert. She was the one who told me to never match art with my couch—and I've held onto this. Even today, I know she knows crap about a bunch of topics she loves to pontificate about, but *she knows Art.*

I give her that.

In her widowhood, my mom let young church women flock to her, offering them good advice on marriage—which always cracked me up a little. It seemed to me—still single, totally hopeless, and COMPLETELY bitter—kinda nutty that my mother, a powerhouse of a woman who pretty much bowed to *no one*—had a bunch of groupies listening to her on marriage when my mom had not exactly been the picture of Submissive Wife.

Kids Without Horses

(The groupies were girls in white, flowing linen dresses with green garlands and yellow daisies wreathed around their heads, and they sat at her feet and asked her to pour out her godly wisdom on their meek and modest souls. Meanwhile, I—brain-damaged and orphaned and planning on a lifetime of being alone—combed through my father's old rock 'n' roll cassettes. Eager to reclaim my boogie shoes—*stop laughing*—I think I was trying very hard to feel okay at rock concerts. It didn't fully work, but in a very short period of time I saw Neil Young, Paul McCartney, Bruce Springsteen, and Stevie Nicks. I never—not once—included myself in the company of those girls at her feet. I was, like, *I'll be damned if I'm putting on a garland.*

Somehow, early on, my mom's counsel was demarcated as something for *other* women, not me.

My mom paid many tributes to her late husband, such that his memory was cherished and his faults were glossed over. Some bad things about him died with him. She took her wedding ring and engagement ring and designed a new piece of jewelry that she wore on her finger. (I was never happy about this.)

My dad was here for September 11, though it's like he missed its permanence, its mold. He never took his shoes off at an airport.

My dad missed Hurricane Katrina.

My dad missed the birth of my kids, his grandchildren.

My dad missed the deaths of Michael Jackson, David Bowie, Robin Williams.

My dad missed the publication of all of my books.

My dad missed Facebook.

My dad missed the election of the first Black man as President of the United States.

My dad missed my cancer.

My dad missed the aging of my mother.

My dad missed the Trump presidency.

My dad missed *The Office*.

He didn't get to see how Wendy looks just like him.

My dad missed every complication of my real life, the one where I became this real woman who had her own family, her own sensibility, her own virtues and crime streaks. He would never see me step out of my insecurities as a young and damaged adult. He would never know that I'd climb mountains again or get a little bad-ass in tight situations.

He'd never know that I'm not really bitter anymore.
Damn, Dad, you'd love my dog.

* * *

Were we death-haunted, the two of us, my mom and I?

I mean, we *were*.

Of course we were.

This was all before social media and maybe there were smartphones, but I didn't have one—so the details are pulled from an unruly, brain-damaged memory. It was the summer of 2003. (Apparently, the smartphone got crazy popular around 2007. I doubt we had flip phones on that trip.)

My dad had been dead for almost a year.

I was thirty-three, single, and Tim was not in the picture yet.

My mom was fifty-seven. Hard to imagine. Widowed for one year, going to Ireland with her daughter to attend her daughter's friends' wedding, because, *yes*, death haunted us both, *chased us*: the bell possibly tolling behind us, over us, like a boulder rolling on our tails as if we were Indiana Jones. The bell tolled *so loudly*, and we had to run. She never imagined this life—nor did I.

It's hard to imagine either of us any more alone than we were then.

I will only speak for myself. (I'm sure her inner sanctimony would now demand that she say that she was *never* alone. *She always felt the presence of God.*)

I was so alone. I'd buy a house down the street, but I did so out of resignation—not with joy. I'd move into my rightful place as an adult, accepting my fate and its isolation. As I think back on my teaching profession, I realize I never had any passion for it. *Never*. I taught, so I could write. *That* was what I really was passionate about. (Career ambition entirely eluded me. *I just wanted to write*.) Marriage would never happen, I assumed. It wasn't in my realm of possibilities. I'd get some cats. Which I did.

My friends stuck with me. Two, especially, in town. But I can't imagine that I was much fun. I can't imagine that I offered much of anything, frankly. Not great conversation. They certainly couldn't share their woes with me. How do you bitch about single life or your love life or your professional path or even your rent with someone living with her mom who just got her driver's license again? I wasn't confident or witty or interesting or adventurous or sensitive or even a "good ear." I was their "good deed," a philanthropic act of humanity.

(For the record, I'm still friends with these two . . . and I think that I eventually resumed personhood—but there were years of toddling along. *Did we go out to eat? Did we see movies? Did I tell a good joke?*)

Julie, the bride in Ireland, was my first post-Accident real friend. We had gotten our MFA degrees together at Arizona State, and that was the only true arena in which I stood on equal footing with others. (Elsewhere: I was the *Lesser Christian*, the *Lesser Woman*, the *Lesser EVERYTHING*.)

Julie and I were writers together, and, um, *I was pretty good.*

But so was she!

Yeah, we'd go to Julie and Bob's (R. Dean Johnson's) wedding in Ireland. I'm a little floored now at our spontaneity, which seems to have eluded both of us nowadays.

But we went.

* * *

Oh, Marilynn Spiegel had other moments of spontaneity!

Sidney Poitier died as I was writing this, in January 2022.

My mom and Sidney went *way* back.

The story goes that my mom suntanned on the Bahaman beach in Nassau next to Poitier during her honeymoon with my dad in the late 1960s. (Poitier would've already been in his late forties and he apparently was still *hot* . . . .) Like, my mom saw him there in the golden sand, and she spread out her beach towel next to him.

Who could muster up the vim to spread out their towel next to Sidney Poitier?

To stand in the warm sand—maybe casting a long shadow—right next to his gorgeous brown bod by the ocean, whipping a hotel beach towel up into the air like a sail, gently smoothing it over the coast, spreading her undoubtedly bikinied body over it, right next to Sidney Poitier?

Who could do that?

My mom could.

My mom would.

* * *

Kids Without Horses

I saved a *New York Times* article dated November 13, 1996, that I must've clipped in Manhattan, because I was living there then (pre-Accident, Dad alive). It was about the wild horses in the Dublin projects; the horses would soon to be prohibited and confiscated.

The Ballymun Flats were the Dublin projects, the ghetto. Seven towers stood in the Ballymun Flats, each named after a 1916 Easter Rising leader. At the Rising, Ireland had sought independence from England, but the rebellion had been unsuccessful. No independence for Ireland. *I see seven towers, but I only see one way out,* U2 sang on the 1987 song, "Running to Stand Still." Seven towers, Dublin poverty, a heroin epidemic—and wild horses, cared for by the impoverished Ballymun kids.

An unforgettable image, really.

There was criticism surrounding the removal of the horses, even though the horses were often abandoned and bony, starved or impoverished like their makeshift owners.

What would happen to those kids without horses?

The heroin epidemic raged.

I tried to find out what happened later. I couldn't find a thing. The Ballymun Flats were torn down between 2004–07. I know nothing about the kids.

Something about this made me call a fictional story by that title.

* * *

What had I been thinking? Was it the unsuccessful bid for independence at the heart of the Rising? The refuge that hopeless children sought in caring for wild beasts?

But there was another story, too—another origin story. I had saved clippings of that one as well. I had clipped a story about kids beating an old horse to death with sticks and bats in Silbee, Texas, on September 14, 1995, leaving the dead horse in a mess of a barbed wire fence. (I was still in New York when I discovered this.) The horse was named Mr. Wilson Boy. In my fictional version, barbed wire was threaded through his nostrils.

A true story about a horse killed.

Even writing this down in 2022 still makes my heart pulse oddly.

I don't know what happened to those kids in Texas, just like I don't know what happened to the Irish boys. The news was carried all over the place. Were their lives destroyed? *Do I want for them to have been destroyed?*

Kids Without Horses

Somehow, in my mind, the wild horses of Ballymun Flats and the dead horse with the barbed wire in Texas worked together and led to "Kids Without Horses."

* * *

Before I publish this, must my mom be dead?

Please note that she was the one who said it first, *Publish it when I'm dead.*

The truth is this: I'm not expecting to live long myself. I'm a bit of a time bomb.

If it's not brain damage, it's cancer.

If it's not cancer, it's a meningioma.

Shockingly, as of this writing, I still haven't gotten Covid.

(*Wait. I got it in July 2022!*)

Nonetheless: *I made my peace with a short life.*

I'm putting my house in order.

But with my mom: *No peace as of this writing.*

What I believe is that the end really matters. It matters so much. And I'm not sure that I'll actually ever make peace with my mom. It might not happen. (I was just reading Ann Patchett's book, *These Precious Days*, and she was talking about her friendship with this woman dying of cancer, and how she cared for her—massaging her legs. And I was thinking how I want to be there for my mom. I want to be able to take care of her. I really, really do—but could I *massage her legs*?) I'm not sure I'll stop being the person I am with her, and I don't really think she'll stop being the person she is with me.

Something happened.

Something in that exchange at the door right after my father died instantly. When she said, *Please don't leave me.*

Something that built upon another tragic moment when the fifty-two-year-old woman flew across the world to pick up her twenty-eight-year-old daughter from an international hostel, where the daughter was living.

It was before Trump. (He was just the nail in the coffin.)

We had upset the natural balance. We had upset the mother-daughter equilibrium one too many times.

Let me go all James Joyce, all stream of consciousness, for a bit.

Kids Without Horses

We had upset the mother-daughter equilibrium one too many times, yes....

First, when my adulthood was snatched away from me in South Africa in 1998 when Nelson Mandela still reigned.

First, when she found me, when she landed on foreign soil to take her brain-damaged daughter home.

Her daughter, not exactly bloodstained but bruised nonetheless, childlike but entrenched in this weird, faux-expatriate life, this endless summer camp, this Cape Town White Girl Melodrama set to the Verve singing "Bittersweet Symphony": *I'm a million different people from one day to the next.*

That daughter.

She found me there, damaged *permanently*, in the arms of a hot guy who was, like, *Yeah, please take her out of here.*

My mother found me, a twenty-eight-year-old expat adventurer, forever rendered *messed up.*

Hot guy, be gone! Expat no more! Get thee home!

Oh, baby, baby, it's a wild world, and I'll always remember you like a child, girl.*

We had upset the balance.

Second, when I was on the cusp, the edge, of reclaiming my sense of self, my personal Stevie Nicksness (I'm full of rock 'n' roll venom today), my writer badge, my father died instantly in a car crash on Bell Road and my mother said, *Please don't leave.*

We had upset the balance.

Mother-daughter, daughter-mother, friends, enemies, needy, independent.

But neither of us was going to succumb; neither of us was going to go down without a fight.

She would mother me, smother me, beam with pride at my accomplishments, cower in shame at my indiscretions, talk me up to strangers, make excuses for me to her friends, never let me go.

I'd rely on her, call on her, let her in on my secrets, and cut her loose when I was done.

We had upset the balance.

Now, decades later, it's all shaky ground.

Holy Ground?

We are not nice people together.

---

*From Cat Stevens' "Wild World."

But maybe I'll reconcile myself with my mother. Can I do it before I actually lose her?

* * *

So we went to Ireland in July 2003. Of course—*but of course!*—we stayed at the Clarence on 6–8 Wellington Quay, the Bono-and-Edge-owned hotel (at least back then). Minimalist, outrageously expensive, stark but chic, with a fabulous location along the River Liffey in the Temple Bar district. What I remember about the hotel was that it was uber-metropolitan, we were jet-lagged and slept wildly, and we ate dinner at the Clarence in a posh dining room. It was sparse, clean, with cute Irish guys at the front desk. I've always been a sucker for cute Irish guys, both before my brains were bashed in *and* after.

Oh, Ireland!

My mom and I would have two international trips before I married Tim and before I slowly but surely disassociated from her. First, Ireland. We had an amazing time. I only think of her in Ireland in a good light. My memories are not harsh. She is young and in shape, and she drove the whole time because there was no way in hell I could drive on the wrong side of the road. (*At what point, I wonder now, did I start being the one who insisted upon driving us places? At what point, I wonder now, did I tell her that she wasn't allowed to drive my kids anywhere?*) She drove on the wrong side of the road, the two of us laughing, sometimes on absurdly narrow two-way streets on steep cliffs with sheep crossing the road or on a slice of rugged coast on the Beara Peninsula near a fishing village—sometimes seriously just having had Irish coffees with Bailey's in a pub minutes before. A drink of whisky for us? This sounds so absurdly unlike either of us, her anxiety-ridden and law-abiding and a venomous hater of reckless abandon, and me—high-strung, a control freak, and a full-fledged teetotaler. Who were we back then, two decades ago? And how did we ever get along?

And then we went to Cuba together, as part of my job at a small college. I took my mother on my educational visa. We had a blast.

What happened?

I can't even go out to breakfast with her without feeling like crap.

* * *

Kids Without Horses

This is the part that I can't let her read, the part that requires me to publish the book *after* she dies. Knowing her, she'll live well-past one hundred.

I'll write her a letter.

Dear Mom,

What happened? What happened to us?

I've cooked up a theory in my head, and I believe it to be true. I'm so sorry. *I believe it is true.*

I left you, and you didn't leave me.

Sometimes, I think it was at the side of your bed in the rehab hospital after your botched hip surgery. When I sat there on my laptop, not even interacting with you, because I just wanted a rest from my sad, sad life. Maybe it was then, then, when you saw that I was there but absent.

I left.

Maybe it was another time, though.

In the beginning, when Tim and I were just married and everything was so horrible, I had a sense that he'd want to move out-of-state at some point. I knew I had to keep him in Arizona. I had to, because I *never* wanted to go anywhere alone with him. *It was unimaginable.* That he would be my only *friend*? That I'd rely on *him*?

I was still dependent on you.

My mother.

Later, though, at the married-for-a-while point, when the sorrow had passed, the codependency kicked-in. The you-are-my-world psychosis took over in our marriage.

When he brought up moving with more vigor later, I thought, *Yeah, that might be fun!*

Yeah, that might be fun!

By then, he was my world.

I'd go with him.

My friend.

My tragic soulmate who I couldn't possibly live without.

Had I squeezed you out?

(You see, mom, I am not like you. When dad died, you carried the hell on. But I am terrified of outliving Tim. Even writing it down frightens me. I'm afraid that God might hear me and want to show me how to deal, how to rise to the occasion, and *I don't want to.* I don't want to deal. *So, God,* I think, *let's forget I mentioned it.*)

But there's another part of my theory. I've been married now for about eighteen years. I know I'm crazy. I know I'm a Type-A person who likes things in a particular way. The dishes in the dishwasher need to be loaded *just* so. I only put my keys down in one of two places; *I don't lose my keys*. I probably have OCD, though I'm undiagnosed. I don't maniacally count or color coordinate closets, and my bookshelves are a nightmare to behold—but I wash my hands *a lot*. You never need to worry about whether or not I washed my hands after going to the bathroom (*I did*). My craziness is multilayered. I can burn, I can rage. A brain injury was an insult to my intelligence. Do you think I will kowtow to a little cognitive damage? *I think not.*

Crazy.

I know that marriage tempers me. I'm not allowed to be as crazy as I might be. I have a built-in crazy odometer called *Tim Bell* (also crazy, but *differently*).

This is one real function of marriage: *One doesn't get to be as crazy as one might be.*

You gotta keep your cool when you're married.

You don't get to let loose.

Marriage tempers you.

That other person—even if he's nuts, too—is there to, figuratively speaking, move you *off* the crazy stove-top burner and place you on the *other* burner. The cooled-off one.

You know what I mean?

Through no fault of your own, Mom, you don't have that.

There is nothing to stop your crazy.

And, Dear Lord, your *intemperance* is staggering.

Staggering.

Death-defying.

There is no one in your house 24/7, saying, *You can't say that . . .* or *Well, I don't know if you're right about that . . .* or *It might actually mean something else.*

That human buffer.

The person who tells you, *Calm down.*

Keep your shit together.

There are things you, Mom, say that no tempered person says.

Is it standing up for what you believe or raging like a lunatic?

Is it being full of vim and vigor or burning down the house?

Is it telling it like it is or gossip?

Is it a Christian revival or reckless abandon?

Is it the local news report or doomsday rants that are antithetical to postmillennial eschatology?

Is it a belief in things not seen or cynicism?

Kids Without Horses

And, at some point—*I don't even know when*—I said to myself, *Enough is enough.*

Enough is freakin' enough.

At some point, I said to myself, *I'm not a child.*

I remember, once, being in your house and I was, like, in my forties, and there were a bunch of old church friends present, like a reunion of sorts, and you scolded me for not sharing the Doctrine of Exclusive Psalmody anymore—and I paused, wondering if you thought it was cute to banter like that in public. Like, *did you think it amused people?* And did you think I was simply wrong and you were simply right because you were clear thinking, while I subscribed to—*what?*—a Social Gospel?

Did you still have a job to do—the job of correcting my thinking?

Dear Lord, it was at that moment.

That moment.

I knew the women who were there, but my affection for them waned.

I wouldn't accept that scolding, and I wouldn't be in the posture of a child.

It wasn't cute, and I wouldn't accept that *ever* again.

I do not remember if I stayed there for the rest of the get-together or not; I only know that I decided not to attend any social events with you again. I was middle-aged, and I wasn't going to be treated like a child.

That's what happened.

And, no, no, I no longer want to see our onetime mutual friends, *because I can't. I just can't.* I had to step away. I had to get away.

We are kids without horses now, the both of us.

* * *

Our trip was well documented in photos and maps, but very little in writing. From Phoenix to Newark, and from Newark to Dublin, we arrived on June 27, 2003—the day before my mom's fifty-seventh birthday. We would fly out from Shannon on July 3 for our return trip. I had all kinds of U2-centric plans. We'd go to the Bonovox Hearing Aid Store on Earl Street North, just off O'Connell Street, because that was the inspiration for Paul Hewson's name change. (We made it.) As of this writing, it's still very much in business. We would look for Bono's house, the Edge's house, and Mount

Temple Comprehensive School, where they met as teen boys. (We never made it.) We had boxty pancakes—potato pancakes—which we were into because we are Jews (this will make more sense later) when it comes to food and Irish *latkes* sounded like a plan. We drank plenty of Irish coffee with Bailey's because, well, it's so good.

I created a page in my photo album of the trip that has just a few itinerary notes on it. In the cab from the airport to the Clarence, I asked the cabbie about the Ballymun Flats. I couldn't understand a word he said, except that he told us they were being torn down. He possibly said, I noted on our itinerary, *If we can live with the Protestants, we can live with anything*, and he possibly *also* said something anti-Semitic.

I didn't tell him that we were Protestants *and* Jews. Too confusing.

* * *

Am I making this part up?

Aging 101: Humor and the World Wide Web.

She is already well past those days now—long past her Irish coffee era on the hunt for U2 in Dublin. We had always laughed together, *always*. Growing up, we were this off-color blend of a Christian household, a Jewish household, and a dirty joke or two. I grew up on Woody Allen, till even we had to turn away with a look of disgust. But we were the ones laughing at fart jokes, mildly obscene stories, *Blazing Saddles*, and Eddie Murphy.

But as my mom aged, I noticed a subtle shift.

I've thought a lot about this.

First, her humor gradually changed.

I noticed it initially with, of course, *The Office*.

Yes, *The Office*.

I love *The Office*. I love it dearly. Obsessively. Abnormally. Everybody knows this about me.

And I get that there are non-*Office* people out there; I do.

(I mean, I *get* it, but I don't.)

But my mom wasn't supposed to be a non-*Office* person.

She was supposed to love *The Office*.

But she just *didn't*.

And, yeah, it hit me.

What was this?

A loss of irony?

Why did my mother, who once loved all that edgy stuff, now crave sweet drivel like *Call the Midwife* or the sedate pageantry of *Downton Abbey*? (I like *Downton*, don't get me wrong—but I prefer a little *Better Call Saul*, if you know what I mean.)

What happened to her love of weirdness? Was her *Absurdity Barometer* on the fritz?

Nowadays, she might suggest a sanctimonious disaffection of some sort, an estrangement from the twisted. Her Moral Compass can't stomach my favorites.

(*Curb Your Enthusiasm* makes her anxious, though she admits that my dad would've loved it.)

But I also know she's into the local news with its daily body count, and she could tell you about every serial killer, pedophile, and petty thief within the vicinity. Plus, despite any piety she might pour out on me, she really likes *Succession* and *Peaky Blinders* and *Ozark*.

So it really couldn't be sanctimonious reasons for her non-*Office* habit.

Why did my mom not love The Office?

In my heart of hearts, I thought it was a loss of irony. Yes, so subtle. The nuances of the weird.

That was a sign of aging.

Yeah, some memory stuff was happening. No biggie.

Yeah, she's not especially hustling across any dance floor singing "Stayin' Alive" anymore. No biggie.

Yeah, she's intemperate and thinks she's subtle about her attempts to evangelize my children. But that's not really an aging thing. She's always been like that.

Yeah, she's a harbinger of doom. Aging? Kinda.

But it was really the *loss of irony*.

And the *internet*.

The other sign of aging that crept up on us unexpectedly had to do with, of all things, the internet.

While her humor shifted with aging, so did her relationship with the World Wide Web.

I know we're all addicts, getting increasingly dumber, destroying what little attention span we have so that every single one of us needs ADHD meds, losing our ability to have real relationships with other human beings, and sowing the seeds of Civil War in America.

That's not an aging thing.

(And that's not even Trump's fault! It's Al Gore's!)

But something unique happened to her when our internet went down in January 2022 for not more than four days.

During a supply-chain shortage, due to Biden or Trump or Covid or inflation.

It took a while to get everything repaired.

No internet!

Stop the streaming!

Netflix, Hulu, Amazon Prime: *gone*!

Facebook: *gone*!

I sent my mom a text on the morning after our first night *alone*, "Did you make it?" I asked, jokingly.

"Did I make what?" she responded, not jokingly.

And then I got so sad.

The temporary cessation of a global connection took this jarring toll on her. And we were witness to it.

But also largely immune from it: Tim rigged up a hotspot so we could still work.

However, my old mom suffered.

Her life had already become very stationary. She was no longer going many places. She watched a lot of TV. She met friends for brunch, but there was down-time.

And she, well—this is the tragic part—*lived on social media.*

I always knew that my mother very much enjoyed the role of matron saint, the role of religious pundit, the possessor of Wisdom and Truth. The disapproval I had always felt from her was built on this.

It came from a particular place in her.

She was, undoubtedly, a good Christian woman.

Now, an old woman, widowed, mostly immobile, she couldn't help it.

What more could she do than share the Gift of God?

On Facebook!

Social media became her pulpit.

Facebook sermons, Bible verses, and righteous politics. Eschatology, Exclusive Psalmody, doctrine. (You name it, she's got it.)

Her very identity was threatened by the loss of the internet.

The lack of the web was not easy on her.

I wouldn't say that she *crumbled.*

Teetered?

Trembled?

Was *humbled?*

We were there for her, okay?

We were there.

We were there, but . . . she was a bit lost.

Was it my imagination or did she become *frailer* in those few off-the-grid days?

How much did she age?

Was she, after all, more like Tim's elderly mom—secluded in her bedroom watching TV reruns of the *Andy Griffith* ilk and avoiding the ice on the steps—than I knew?

What did it feel like to be her?

To feel that community she had on Facebook dry up instantly so that all that she had was her reprobate daughter and her *Looney Tunes* son-in-law upon whom she really had no other choice but to depend?

The community with their affirmations and her pontification platform had slipped away.

It was just her, an old woman.

And her daughter, who was worldly and went grocery shopping on Sunday and voted for Biden.

* * *

Dublin was a mad dash. The Clarence was luxurious. Trinity College and the Book of Kells. Bewley's Oriental Café, established in 1840 (I think they dropped the *Oriental* part). St. Stephen's Green, Fitzwilliam Square, Merrion Square. Rainbow-bright doors and walk-up flats. I pictured myself as an Irish Bridget Jones, dating eligible bachelors with accents, living in an adorable flat, wearing short skirts (*I'd be taller, slimmer*), carrying a briefcase (*more professional*—or *someone else altogether*). An afternoon Bailey's Irish Coffee (the very first one) at Café en Seine and a stroll along Grafton Street, crossing the River Liffey on the Ha'Penny Bridge, wandering around the Winding Staircase Bookstore, and taking pictures at the Bonovox Hearing Aid Store off of O'Connell Street. Apparently, I bought a CD of U2 cover songs at Mojo's Records in Temple Bar. I do not think I've seen that CD in my possession since that day.

(I guess I wanted to meet Bono in order to be permanently destroyed by the havoc visited upon those who meet their heroes.)

Where did that CD go?
Along with my relationship with my mother?

We visited Christ Church Cathedral, St. Patrick's Cathedral, Parnell Square/Garden of Remembrance, a modern art museum, and some kind of Vegas-style *Riverdance* show.

After two nights in Dublin, we picked up a rental car and drove all day on the wrong side of the road, stopping at Powerscourt Gardens. I wrote of Powerscourt: *A beautiful spot, nearly worth risking our lives to get to.* The plan was to head over later to Kilkenny.

We got absurdly lost trying to get there. The story goes that we pulled over at a random little cottage somewhere in Southern Ireland, where I walked up to the door of a home along a lush and winding pathway, knocked, and said to the puzzled Irishman who answered, "I'm sorry to bother you, but I wonder if you could tell me how to get to Kilkenny?"

This was about as weird as someone showing up at one's Phoenix condo and asking a random dude how to get to Reno.

* * *

When Y2K was approaching, I didn't really care. It was only a few years after "The Accident," and I lived with my parents—I'd turn thirty right before the world ended—and maybe I welcomed cataclysm.

My dad was still alive, and I think he cared about Y2K a little more than I did.

My mom was obsessed.

She filled the hall closet with food that astronauts ate.

Gallons of purified bottled water lined the shelves in the laundry room.

She had a clean blue recycler bin filled with more water and sealed up in the back shed—specifically to be used for bathing later, in the new century, when it would be scarce. I never knew what happened to that blue bin later—I never asked her—but I know that the astronaut food was still there in 2015, when my mom finally moved out. (Did she still have some in the addition?)

Before the clocks turned and the apocalypse possibly began, my parents had gone to bed around ten at night—despite imminent danger—and I had watched the Gin Blossoms perform downtown on a local Phoenix TV channel. I had lounged on my parents' couch in my childhood home, where I still live now in some kind of warped non-Oedipal Shakespearean tragedy. I had worn a bulky mauve robe to bring in the new century, I was in an MFA program doing the only thing I have ever done well, I was a woman devoted to "ER" and "Third Watch" because the Television Renaissance had only just begun, and I was wholeheartedly cynical about anything happening as exciting as all the computers of the world shutting down and the planet going black.

As the epoch gave way, I—prone, alone, and a stereotype—stretched my toes in my socks, and thought, *Nothing's happening.*

Hey, jealousy! sang the Gin Blossoms.

I was already your basic Kid Without a Horse.

* * *

At some point, we switched to decaf Bailey's in our Irish Adventure, which cracks me up. We gave up the caffeine, but not the whiskey!

We toured the Waterford Crystal Factory.

I have no clue why there are no photos of us at Blarney Castle (where we, at least, stood nearby while *others* kissed the Blarney Stone). No proof exists.

There were other castles, as well.

We went to Kinsale, where there were two pubs we liked: The Mad Monk and Jim Edwards'. We both bought expensive art that I still have (and love) at Gallery Catoire.

From County Cork, we headed to County Kerry. We went around the Beara Peninsula and what I called *the beautiful but treacherous* Healy Pass in the scanty itinerary notes. Mountain goats peppered the terrain, often with blue paint marking their heads like baptismal splatters to indicate ownership. We detoured to Castletownbere, a coastal town on the Peninsula, a past haven for smugglers. There was none of the sophistication of the Clarence and none of the Emerald Isle Charm of the cottages on the road to Kilkenny. The sky was beautiful but gray, and the fishing trawlers were rusty and smelly.

In Castletownbere, we found a pub. There were women there, and we heard Gaelic (Irish). We watched, fascinated by the locals. The Irishwomen laughed a lot. They were mostly a plain bunch with hair pulled off their faces, occasional chipped teeth, blue jeans, strollers, cigarettes. Had they ever been outside of Castetownbere? Did they long to be somewhere else?

And where did they get their strollers?

Were they like me? Did they long to be Irish Bridget Joneses, working at fashion magazines, dating eligible bachelors who had rock-star fantasies, living in adorable flats, having single female friends, wearing short skirts, carrying little briefcases?

There were children with these women. Boys, little and *tough*. They climbed on top of the picnic tables and stomped on their surfaces. They were into trucks, and they pushed each other while their mothers laughed nearby.

My mom and I loved it all.

We were like that. *People who watched.*

Then, onto Kenmare, our destination for the wedding.

That first night there, I ate monkfish in goat cheese sauce at the Horseshoe. It sounds great, but I'm too old now to remember what it was like.

We stayed at a place called Tara Farm, and there was nothing *not* beautiful about the place called Tara Farm, somewhere near Kenmare. While we did wedding things, we also went to Muckross House in Killarney.

A guide told us how the family living there during the reign of Queen Victoria had been given six year's notice for a two-day visit by the Queen, and the owners spent the next six years preparing—in expectation of a title endowment.

Queen Victoria came and had a lovely time in Kerry. When she left, though, her husband, Prince Albert, took ill and died.

Preoccupied, the Queen forgot about giving away any titles. Financially in trouble after the Muckross renovations in anticipation of the Queen, and without the virtue of being *Sirs* or *Lords*, the Muckross owners were obligated to sell.

History, made. Never what's expected.

Bob and Julie were married in a little Irish church; there was dinner at the Lime Tree Restaurant (the menu still looks awesome), and they had their first dance in a pub.

Can you say *perfect*?

Why they actually chose me to be there, I'll never really know; I do know that I think of it as a treasure.

* * *

Kids Without Horses

My mom and I don't seem to have much in common anymore. We both love animals. We're both OCD (she'd disagree—but, *Dear Lord*, we are). We're both kinda like *It's my way or the highway* (again, she'd disagree). We both like art. We're both pretty intense about our lives as moms, even if neither of us is the best (I suspect that she thinks she really *is* the best). We're both not racists (though she says outdated things, I know she's not a racist). We both romanticize the epicness of our lives. We're both City Girls. We both like chocolate.

Religion?

I suspect—I *know*—she thinks me a heretic. Even though I was raised as a staunch Calvinist with the Right Doctrine, I somehow embraced a Social Gospel, she'd say. Sometimes, when she's mad at me, she tells me that her friends ask if everything is okay with me, like maybe I'm off my rocker.

She thinks I married well (though Tim is nuts, we match). She loves my kids. She loves my dog. She asks me for TV recommendations.

She wishes I dressed nicely. I'm a *schlub*; something happened to make me not *care*. She wishes I were more genteel and I liked nice restaurants. I no longer see the value of seared asparagus and other seared delicacies. She wishes I went to Bible studies and church potlucks. She thinks Tim and I live it up and waste money. She imagines we eat tons of fried food and pasta. She tries to deliver messages under the table to my kids about Christianity. Hopefully, they'll see the Light!

She eats dinner for breakfast. (She always has!)

She buys potato chips on the lowdown.

I think I got my rock 'n' roll and book-love from my dad, but I think she'd say the literary thing is from her. She did attend a Bruce Springsteen concert with me after 9/11, but I never hear her listening to music.

We are different, and I suppose she'd attribute the differences to my lack of orthodoxy.

I'd say that I just grew up and became *me*. The epicness of my life did its work on me. Profound injury created a *before* and *after*.

* * *

The early death of her husband caused her to skip middle age.

I, too, skipped middle age.

We have that in common.

Kids Without Horses

* * *

After the wedding in Kenmare, we were off again!

We stopped in Limerick to pay tribute to Frank McCourt.

Somewhere on the road, we got food. My mom ordered "Linda McCartney's Vegetarian Breakfast," which she swore was good, despite what looked like canned beans and tofu sausages.

Bunratty Castle stayed with the both of us.

When one thinks of Bunratty, one thinks of Vikings and a fortress and the whole moat thing. A drawbridge.

History exists there in a way that just eludes Americans. First, it was a Norman fortress in 1250. Then, in the 1400s, after wreckage and strife, it became a castle—because medieval castles were all the rage. *Earls* were involved. Three main floors, I think. Four towers.

I was mostly interested in how they used the toilet—like feces, like *What happened with poop?*

Hadn't I heard that royal people just peed in the corners of Versailles?

No toilet paper?

No incessant handwashing?

I mean, what does one do if one is three floors up, it's in the middle of the night, the stairs are cold blocks of rock, and the halls are dank echo chambers that smell moldy or like the zoo? Did one really toss the crap out the window and try to hit the water in the moat? *Really?*

Let's not even talk about B.O.

(But we can, if you want.)

I remember us climbing spiral staircases between floors, huffing and puffing, red-faced, trying to catch our breath, laughing so hard, because we couldn't believe this medieval life—This Wild Medieval Life!—and I had to go to the bathroom like I always do, but we kept laughing and I said, *I'm going to pee in my pants if we don't get out of here*, though the only way down was through banquet halls and chapels and kitchens containing dead rabbits for stew and the many, many staircases undoubtedly leading to a dungeon or the River of Poo.

We were laughing so hard.

And I never peed my pants because we found Durty Nelly's, a pub dating back to 1620, that had seafood chowder, soda bread, and—*for sure, for sure*—Bailey's and coffee.

Always, with the Bailey's and coffee

Crazily, ironically, on that very same day, we went to the Cliffs of Moher in County Clare. This place of ravishing, pure beauty.

It's the site where we took the only existing photo of us together in Ireland.

* * *

My mom did amazing things over our lifetime together. Never bitter. I wonder if she knows that this is *the thing*—not her wisdom or ministries or the purity of her faith—but *this* that I admire most.

I know I've been cripplingly bitter at times in my life, after a lousy relationship, post-Accident, during my marriage, over my lackluster book sales.

I know that she also taught me how to survive. She mourned; I saw profound sorrow. But she literally picked herself up off the ground. She looked at her life. She said, "Okay, Lord," like Abraham or Moses (no joke)—and she got to her feet, got a job, started walking the dog since my dad wasn't going to do it, morphed into a new role in her church circle, and got savvy on the internet (relatively speaking). She edged into the Scottsdale Art Scene. She hobnobbed with artists. She was closer to her sister. She ate expensive Thai.

She never once held me back after "The Accident." Disapproval came later.

She stood by me in pursuing a writing career (like, *is that even done anymore?*).

She stood by me when I bought a new house.

She came over at 10 p.m. (the new midnight) when my kitten broke his leg and I was flipping out.

She gave my books to her friends, beaming in pride, even though I wrote crazy stuff with bad words.

She threw me a wedding when I married on whim.

She rushed to the hospital to see my first baby, and she came over to take care of my toddler when we went to have our second baby.

She tried to be there when my marriage looked like it would collapse.

She loved my husband when I said, *He's good to go again*.

She lives in her little "casita," wondering why I don't text, and she loves her cat as if Scout were a deity, and she eats salad for breakfast, watching *Masterpiece Theatre*. She still gets the mail every day and shops at Safeway, even though it's overpriced. She has friends for brunches and games and fancy early dinners, and the Facebook algorithms suit her style. She doesn't recycle, but she might use an ATM machine now. She could probably teach the police a thing or two.

But she never got bitter.

Not once.

* * *

On that last night in 2003, we went to Doolin.

The town to go to for traditional Irish music.

And there we were, loving every second of it. Doolin was rural, and I wrote: *Closest thing to the Transkei in South Africa that I've ever seen.* Ireland was like Africa! That isolated, hushed, vast, beauty.

My mom may have been one of the oldest people on the streets of Doolin after dark.

We spent an afternoon writing postcards, drinking more Bailey's and coffee, talking to farm animals, and eating fish 'n' chips in Gus O'Connoll's Pub on Fisherstreet. When it was late, we listened to live traditional Irish music. There were traditional instruments like the fiddle and someone bringing down the house with a zither.

I think it was a zither.

Some backpacker from Calgary brought his drums.

Sweet, sweet Doolin!

I miss it as I write it.

We flew out of Shannon in the morning.

* * *

I do not think that my mom and I will ever have our Moment of Truth. She will never get that thing she hopes for. She will never get what she craves, that moment I look her deep into her eyes and finally—*finally!*—say, *You were right all along. Thank you!*

She will imagine me arriving at Heaven's gate, and it won't be Saint Peter welcoming me—since we're Protestants—but Jesus Himself, who will beckon me over with a kind but firm word: *Your mother knew what she was talking about.*

And I will never get my moment, either.

Kids Without Horses

I never got it with my father. He never survived to see any of this, my real life.

Dad, I passed on our toe-thumb to one of my daughters.

Oh, well. He's with Mr. Rogers and Johnny Cash now.

I think my mom, though, lost both of us. She lost my father. Then, she lost me.

I'm still here, Mom.

But will either of us ever see beyond the Ballymun Flats, the seven towers, the trash caught in weeds, the wreckage and glass shards and relics of sorrow?

So, I end here. With drama. With the image of the kids without horses.

What became of them?

They were only children.

Did they grow old, the images of those beautiful beasts fading? Do they only see the wreckage? How strong are their memories?

At the end of the day, we are those kids.

Kids without horses.

II

John Krasinski Is a Superstar

He is.

A global pandemic hit the planet at some mysterious point at the end of 2019 and stopped the world by the spring of 2020. Krasinski—apparently feeling a vacuum in our cultural disposition (Earthlings were not doing well)—launched a YouTube series called Some Good News. *It featured good news. My family loved it.*

There were ways we made ourselves happy, and there were tragedies we couldn't quite forget, despite Tiger King *and the, um, adrenaline rush of racing through empty grocery store aisles in hazmat suits. I think the death of George Floyd rendered the cultural distractions trite, however.*

It was a tough time. Always remember that John Krasinski is a superstar, though.

I wrote this over the course of the pandemic, in 2020 and 2021.

John Krasinski Is a Superstar (2020–21)

Remember *The Blue Lagoon* with Brooke Shields and that guy? How you hypothesized with your best friend about with whom you'd like to be stuck on a deserted island? You were only ten, so who could it have been? Andy Gibb? B.J. and the Bear? Did you want the Bear to join you, too?

Did you ever picture your deserted island like this? With these people? In this sort of landscape?

What do your home, your rooms, your walls—the stained grout of your kitchen tile, the Soviet *matryoshka* dolls and the Desmond Tutu doll and your dusty books and all of the objects you treasure and love on your living room shelves mean to you now in this urban exile?

Do you have enough toilet paper? Coffee? Fancy Feast?

Are you among intimates or strangers? Are you and your husband capable of being trapped alone together? Are you ever alone? Never alone? Do you know people who are alone?

What do you think it's like for them? Do they take certain risks that you don't? Is their isolation more acute than yours? Are you soft in your comfort, shallow in your perceptions? Do you take your family for granted?

How much pleasure are you allowed to experience while those around you suffer?

Did you ever picture yourself hoarding cat litter? Would you risk your life for a pet? Is your dog now allowed on the couch? Don't you want him there, with you, always, stinky, sweet?

Do you have Amazon Prime? Do you watch *Parks and Rec* with the kids? *Criminal Minds*?

Will this be the last time your children really want to be with you? Will you and your husband romanticize this time with them for the rest of your lives? Are your kids in that gentle spot, not babies and not yet teenagers? Do they love you so much, *so very much*? Do you just want to stay locked up in the house, united with the world virtually but not literally, so it's you and your family and no one else, *inexcusably*?

Inexcusably?

Are you vacillating between the purest of the joys, an unadulterated rapture, of having your babies gathered to you, tethered to you, dependent on you, so very *yours* and *yours* and *yours*—and its opposite, end-of-the-world *panic*?

Might this be a Biblical plague?

Bats instead of locusts?

Is this the apocalypse?

Are you supposed to be alive for this? Didn't you already have your crazy? Wasn't your crazy so *crazy*? How much *crazy* does one get? Where's your free pass? Hasn't anyone read your novel about a psychotic marriage? You survive breast cancer to die in a plague? Chemo for this? Have we had enough global warming? Couldn't we warm up some more? Can your kids just grow up first? May you please see the final season of *Homeland* before you meet Jesus?

Where's Melania? Who's taking caring of Barron? Do you think they all love each other? Do you think that Trump ever just sits heavily next to Melania on the couch around 9 p.m. and says, "Damn! I ate too much!"?

What about your books? Does this suggest futility in your vocation? Doesn't anyone on the face of this planet want to read about you dying of cancer? Does your "memoir" land DOA? Doesn't that figure? Doesn't the word "memoir" sound fancy?

Are you crazy for being happy sometimes?

Haven't you been social distancing for about five years now?

Don't your kids consider you antisocial anyways? Is this so different?

Who are your friends? Isn't it curious how this impacts friendships? Like, with whom are you keeping in touch? Do you Zoom? Do you sit outside with your college friends (now middle-aged), their dogs running around, drinking coffee? Do you find it odd that your old friends are still your best friends? Does this say something, maybe, disturbing about who you are? No longer capable of "opening up"?

Or does it reveal a kind of fidelity?

But have you dropped other people? Is a freakin' pandemic an excuse to let them *go*? Do you see a plague as a colossal do-over? Do you ever think, "Good riddance"?

But do you notice that some people drop you, too?

Like, is this some kind of reprioritizing, some kind of hierarchical reshuffling? On a global scale?

Do you realize what is truly valuable in this divvying up of cost and value?

Is this the heart of Covid-19?

Do you love certain people breathlessly, hopelessly, riskily?

Does Trader Joe's deliver?

In the beginning, do you find yourself obsessing about the fate of CNN's Chris Cuomo in his narrow basement with his reddish eyes?

Isn't it ironic that your family spent the winter binging *The 100*?

Is Dr. Fauci okay?

Writers, are you writing? Who will read your words, your common words?

Are you the English professor whose class went on spring break in March 2020 and never went back? Do you only think about two students who were in those sabotaged classes? Do you remember The Girl Who Reminded You of Skipper, who was Right to your Left, and how she told you her father was a doctor and all of this was no big deal? Did she give up her European summer vacation plans? Is she one of those nonmask wearers? Does she eventually call for *Law and Order* in Portland and Seattle?

What about the gay kid, the Best Writer in the Class? Do you remember how he told everyone that he's closeted with his parents? What happened to him when he went home? Does he have a good friend, at least one good friend? Are his parents loving, sensitive people? Does he decide to talk to them? Why does he end up doing so poorly in your English class when he was such good writer? What does quarantine—that Sartre-esque *No Exit* state—do to him? Isn't it illegal to ask a student if he's okay, if he needs to talk? HIPAA? FERPA? Didn't you take an oath of office? Swear on your W-2 form?

Do you protest the death of George Floyd? Do you marvel—for a brief and wondrous moment—how you marched together with others, forgoing safety, making a choice? How you marched with other people, right then, right there, in a solemn unity because you knew—*you really knew*—you would stand with them against an evil that could not contain any of you? You marched *together*, and you knew *together*?

Are any of your relationships suffering because of the election? How are you coping?

What should you do when your friend's dad dies of Covid? Will there be a funeral? Will he suffer from lifelong resentment? Will you be there for him?

Or are you too insular now? Too myopic? Too, well, *inexcusably* (that word, again) self-absorbed?

Remember how you didn't get the anguish of losing a parent till your own father died?

What do you do with the good memories of this pandemic that you guiltily possess? Does your family vacation in A-frame cabins in the woods? Does your family hike and count deer in the forest? Does your family eat gourmet pizza with big dollops of goat cheese on top while sitting on decks during the sunset?

Do you stay quiet about these things? Hushing up while gurneys line sidewalks in Brooklyn? While men are killed by cops?

How does your reality narrow, sharpen, change and not change?

How will you remember this hotbed of a year—the year that Covid spreads in the mist of your breath, the year that a Black man dies on the ground, the year your people gather, and your humanity seems so true?

III

Love Rescue Me
Entering the Holy of Holies

What unites the five pieces included in this section? They're either about God or sanctuaries or my taste in rock 'n' roll.

This Will Be the Best U2 Essay You've Ever Read . . . and The Longest, Too (2001)

This was once a "real" essay I originally called "Love Rescue Me: Entering the Holy of Holies." It appeared in Image, a Journal of the Arts & Religion, in the summer of 2001—and it had to be one of my earliest publishing credits. I wrote it under false pretenses.

Jesus was a liberal.

That was the opening line of my 2001 essay in a lit journal on my supposedly last U2 concert ever. Provocative. No doubt, I raised eyebrows among my church friends. But I was still youngish. Thirty-one.

I actually don't think I'd say that today. Today, I would say that Jesus is nonpartisan. But I was a kid. Thirty-one. Coming off the Clinton years, right before 9/11. It was a different world.

So I went to a U2 concert in 2001, acting as if I were bidding adieu to my childish groupie ways.

* * *

Between us, my friend Ann and I had seen twenty-four U2 shows by the time we hit the road to see them play in San Diego on April 17, 2001 (I had only seen them seven of those times, which hardly qualifies me as a real groupie). We'd attended shows in Tempe, Phoenix, Las Vegas, Los Angeles, San Diego, Sacramento, Oakland, Chicago, and Cape Town, South Africa. We were card-carrying fans, subscribing to *Propaganda*, their magazine, in order to get early-bird ticket specials. (I probably still have ancient copies buried someplace in the house.) I had about a dozen hard-to-find posters rolled up in my closet. (Inherited from a boyfriend who almost ruined my life, they've moved from house to house, closet to closet, for over thirty

Kids Without Horses

years now. One of Bono still hangs in our laundry room. When my kids were little, they thought it was just a poster of their dad—Bono and Tim do bear a slight resemblance!) Sometimes, I think about selling my posters, but I never would. No way. (Plus, do I really want to find out they're worth *pennies*?) Ann had a U2 tattoo. We were both in the audience for the filming of the concert film, *Rattle and Hum*. I still love that movie, and I own it on VHS. (I do not own a VCR.)

Besides our U2 credentials, we had rock 'n' roll experience. Bruce Springsteen, the Rolling Stones, Sting, others. Captain & Tennille.

Johnny Rotten once spit on Ann!

Now, *that's* saying something.

I considered—for about two minutes—being a rock 'n' roll journalist. No joke. Later that very year, I'd write a review of a Bob Dylan concert for the *Arizona Republic*. I was very, very proud of that one. Me, reviewing Dylan!

But we were calling it quits with U2, terminating the relationship. More on that soon.

What I didn't know then: Ann would be the maid of honor at my wedding in 2004. I'd end up feeling horrible about this, unforgivably so, because I chose Ann—a member of my wack-church over my childhood best friend, the OG in my rock 'n' roll groupie life. (I would later need to ask Laura to forgive me for this betrayal.) Ann and I committed to dumping U2 in some kind of purification ritual, I betrayed my best friend, and Bono was—I promise you—the least of my problems. I know I saw U2 at least two more times after this farewell, despite having given them up (I'm not sure how I managed to bypass my sanctimony to attend—but I did). Eventually, I would leave the wack-church. And I probably haven't spoken to Ann in close to a decade now.

So what I didn't know then: Ann would leave my life, and U2 would stay.

But what I do know now: Despite my faux attempt at "closure" (I guess?), my kids can sing all of the lyrics to "Sunday Bloody Sunday." Some kids grow up on "Rock-a-Bye Baby"; my kids grew up on "Bullet the Blue Sky."

* * *

U2 was *my* thing.

(No one else's.)

In the preteen days, it was Duran Duran: Laura (OG) and I, *Sing Blue Silver*, new romantic/fashion/that-Nagel-crap, heterosexual men in make-up, nonsense, exotica, erotica. Pretty boys were plastered all over my pink bedroom walls, and I possessed an outrageous amount of useless information about their love lives via *Bop* and *Tiger Beat*.

Honk if you remember Julie Anne Friedman, Nick Rhodes' wife.

I'm going to blame Barry H. for what happened next.

He was nineteen to my fourteen. Though no Simon Le Bon or John Taylor, he was cute. Nineteen! (I still know him, so he's probably close to sixty now. *Gulp*.) I liked Barry. As did my friend, Jenifer—who inexplicably spelled her name with one "n."

I mean, she spelled it like this: *Jenifer*!

We were all church kids (pre-wack), but Barry was "old." Jenifer and I, in one of the biggest and most innocent double entendres in world history, would speak in code whenever Barry was present. Like, if he walked into the church sanctuary for the freakin' church potluck with his single-guy contribution of a liter of generic soda, Jenifer With One "N" and I would do some quick wink-wink to each other and speak in code.

Brace yourself.

His code name?

Get ready for it.

The Filling in My Donut.

Yes, Jenifer With One "N" and I called Barry *The Filling in My Donut*.

Barry is *Berry*.

Like one fills one's donut with blue*berry* or straw*berry* or maybe boysen*berry* if one is being all gourmet.

So Jenifer With One "N" might wink at me over the pews and quietly say, *The Filling in My Donut is here.*

Lordy.

"Jennifer?" she'd say.

"What, Jenifer?" I'd respond.

"Look over there, Jennifer." Wink-wink.

I'd look, casually, like a spy, a sleuth, a Charlie's Angel.

"*The Filling in My Donut* has arrived in church," Jenifer With One "N" pantomimed, probably obscenely but innocently.

So I blame Barry, *The Filling in My Donut*, for my U2 Love.

Kids Without Horses

One fine day, in the early- to mid-eighties, Barry casually let me, bona fide Duranie, borrow U2's album, *War*, to—I'll cite him—get me off the "pabulum."

Duran Duran = pabulum.

The Filling in My Donut slipped *War* to me as if it were a pile of unmarked bills.

I gave them a listen.

Enlightenment!

It's almost ridiculous to say, but the album changed my life.

How does that happen?

Why does it happen?

What made me lounge on the yellow carpet—yellow!?!—in my childhood pink bedroom next to my boombox with the U2 cassette inside? Why did I listen so hard?

But I did!

Yellow and pink?

A brilliant, observant, powerhouse album. It was a mess, *yes*, just the way an impressionistic painting might be a mess. If one got close to a Monet, did one see only the pale green and pink licks? What must it take to see the gardens, Giverny, the water, the lily pads?

Did I just compare U2 to Claude Monet?

Damn, girl.

Understand the power of *War*. Here, the teen torn between worldliness and spirituality found poetry and prose. (*Have I been fighting this battle my whole life?*) There would be break-your-heart, burst-your-blood-vessels rock 'n' roll that tackled Psalm Forty, and a world both brutal and hopeful. This was angry but optimistic rock. These were universal dirges. They were not postmodern; they were not nihilistic. In these songs, there were still such things as morality, as good and evil, as redemption and sanctification.

There was nothing like it, and there has been nothing like it since.

The tape shredded in my cassette player.

I had to buy Barry a new copy of *War*.

I bought myself one as well.

And the rest, as they say, is history.

* * *

Love Rescue Me

I didn't meet Ann till I was older, like right before the turn of the century. Ann, independently of me, became a fan in 1987, and I never let her forget that I was an "old" fan while she belonged to the post-*Joshua Tree* club. She insisted that she wasn't one of the bandwagon people.

She said that she felt like the albums *Boy* through *War* were a conversation that she walked into (while I was the one *having* the conversation, mind you), and—upon her U2 discovery—she compared the band to "secular church" for her. Unlike me, she didn't grow up in the Christian church—but something about these guys spoke profoundly to her Gen X desire to change the world. She was not latching onto their subtle Christian worldview, as I certainly was.

It became her thing, too, though. Ann worked in a used record store (Zia Record Exchange, still the best in Phoenix, Arizona) and the now-defunct bookstore chain, B. Dalton, to finance U2 road trips, chasing the band around the West Coast. She famously blew off an opportunity to hug Bono because she preferred the Edge, to whom she once compared to Michelangelo's *David*. (My grown-ass woman self loves this last part.)

We were believers, both of us.

Our own U2 lives happened, then, before we ever met up. Concerts. Bad opening acts. Great opening acts. College. Jobs. Travel. I was very much associated with my love of U2 throughout college and into adult life. I grew up in Arizona when Evan Mecham was the short-lived governor, shrewder than Trump and perhaps crueler—he cancelled the MLK holiday and U2 denounced him. (Bono discusses this in his memoir, *Surrender*, and there was actually a threat on his life the night of a concert I attended in town.) Mecham was impeached, and I was thereby aligned with political liberalism.

U2 even affected my love life.

One moody collegiate late night in what had to be, like, 1989 or 1990, this boy-man/U2-fan who moved me in mysterious ways and later gave me all of his hard-to-find posters, asked—in all seriousness—if my feelings for him were a "Bono Thing." He didn't look like Bono (like Tim does!), nor did he sing, raise white flags, or promote debt forgiveness—but he was *also* in the *Rattle and Hum* movie audience.

(Like Voldemort, we do not say this boy/man's name aloud.)

I'm sure that I insisted, "I love you for *you*."

When he eventually exited my life, he prefaced his departure, "Don't go burning all your U2 CDs."

I may have laughed aloud.
I may have said, "Hey, babe, I wouldn't dream of it."
I probably didn't do either of those things.
But U2 was my thing, not *our* thing, not *his* thing—but *my* thing.
And I still have all the hard-to-find posters!
Sucker!

* * *

But then why were we giving U2 up in April 2001?
I guess, at thirty-one, I was struggling.
I had this awareness that no proper Christian guy would have me due to my leftist leanings, questionable artistry, perpetual cussing, suspicious sexuality (it's not easy vacillating between goody-goody and strong, sexy, single woman), and evident disdain at certain religious practices (I've always sucked at orthodoxy). I mean, I really didn't *like* any proper Christian guys—but, still, I didn't want to end up alone (Christian Girl Conundrum). And, yes, Christianity was a prerequisite for a relationship. Rock 'n' roll, liberalism, Christ-centricity: *I was in for some trouble.* Loving some elusive rock band was probably not helping me to look all spiritual and prudent in Christian Guy Circles.

There were other things, too.
Was I flirting with idolatry? (Christian Girl Question.)
Was this like worshipping false gods? (See above.)
And I was disappointed by the band, too. Philosophically disappointed. Rock 'n' roll used to be visionary, universal. Whether it was "Stairway to Heaven" or "Blowin' in the Wind," the world was once outside of ourselves—a place to be changed, handled gently, not confined to myopic hard edges drawn by our own unskilled hands.

By the turn of the century, rock music was self-absorbed, catchy, if not profound then touching? Songs were personal stories, not universal battle cries.

We lost universality.
What happened to us wanting to change the world?
Remember the Cure? We were "curing" what?
Did we still want to cure anything?
Remember all those songs by the Smiths that somehow captured the human condition?

Remember the inherent irony in Nine Inch Nails' *Pretty Hate Machine*?

Remember when rock 'n' roll was capable of convicting us, rather than just feeding our own narcissism?

Wasn't rock 'n' roll once about something besides romance?

Back in the day, I'd be stuck in my self-important quagmire (I'm *quagmire-prone*); I'd be returning to a dorm room late at night, feeling all morose and probably slighted by a good-looking nineteen-year-old, unaware of my destiny to be so-so in middle age, and it was quite possible that I'd fall to my knees while weeping bitterly and spouting Sappho (I was that kind of girl), ensconced in a melancholic ecstasy that seemed almost like a Catholic saint and, as I fell, I'd hit play on my cassette player and hear a requiem by bands called Tears for Fears or Nirvana (*I'm blurring eras; let me*).

But by 2001, it was over.

While I had been sharpening my skills as witty/bitter/reclusive Manhattanite in the nineties, U2 seemed to be going through a Supermodel Stage. Post-college was a shape-shifting time.

By 2001, Bono was well into his Fly routine.

Feed the world?

We weren't feeding any world.

Contemporary rock was like *Seinfeld*; it was about nothing. Fundamentally—like with *Seinfeld*—we were left *untouched*.

Imagine that: to be left *untouched*.

That TV show (which I faithfully watched) was iconic, archetypal. Were you all that upset when the entire show ended with the gang in jail?

You were not.

Untouched.

And, as I reflected in my thirty-one-year-old "maturity," the U2 love had paralleled my own growth as a woman.

As a Christian teen, U2 was affirmation, an arm around my shoulder, a whisper saying, *This is Christianity; it's raw rock 'n' roll so true that you can't stop listening.* For me, it was political, brutal, honest, a place to rest when I began to squirm in sermons.

As an adult, I was hotheaded with spiritual inclinations and political passions and a penchant for writing in dark rooms. U2 music grounded me.

When I was young and doing young things, U2 was young, too. We were loud, we were banging things, we were shouting. When I was fierce, on fire, protesting, waving white flags, U2 was also fierce, on fire, protesting, waving white flags.

Kids Without Horses

In the nineties, though I was unable to articulate this, I sensed that both of us had sold out. I had sold out; U2 had sold out.

By thirty-one, I was conscious of having sold out.

None of us were changing the world.

How could the world be changed?

In 2000–2001, U2 was singing "Elevation." It wasn't exactly "Sunday Bloody Sunday," but I felt the same way about it as I felt about *Seinfeld*. It was out-of-control appealing, full of spark, more exciting than a Slip 'N Slide in the seventies.

But it was no "Pride (In the Name of Love)."

I should get a divorce.

So, Ann and I declared ourselves *Out*.

* * *

I mentioned the wack-church. That's undoubtedly a bit of a red flag in my prose....

Can I really just leave it at that?

I've written about it before in fiction, but I'm not super interested in full-fledged cult dissection. My husband wants me to write a book.

I guess I'd say that this particular community took Biblical truths and, um, weaponized them?

Used them against others?

Promoted a kind of salvation-by-works, a hard-hearted type of judgmentalism masked in intellectualism?

Dear Lord, my own verbiage is creeping me out!

But Tim and I fled with the kids a little more than a decade after that San Diego U2 concert. We fled for our lives—and I know I've said this elsewhere: We fled like Dustin Hoffman and Katharine Ross fled the church in *The Graduate*. We hopped a bus, sat in the back, and looked stunned. Maybe Simon and Garfunkel music played in the background.

We were free.

* * *

In 2001, on the Elevation Tour, Ann and I had floor tickets at the San Diego Sports Arena (the arena had been featured in that great movie, *Almost Famous*). Right in the front was a big heart shape whose outline encompassed the entire stage. Only three-hundred people were "allowed" into its well-guarded confines. Both the stage and the special U2 people were within the heart's walls. Bono could run around the top of the heart, people inside.

It was the Holy of Holies.

We were in line early for the first wristband to try to get into the heart. The methodology of heart access is still enigmatic to me. I just did what Ann told me to do. Basically, it can be summed up like this: *Go for the heart*.

Which, of course, we successfully did.

We went straight for the heart, and we made it.

* * *

Did I mention that Ann was a philosophy professor? Two college professors! How insane is that?

She was very philosophical (I was just trying to snag a nice guy).

She spoke of giving U2 up, because, she said, "I'm in love with reality."

(*Cult.*)

That sounded very profound to me.

(*Cult.*)

U2's "selling-out," its mass marketing, its forsaking of ballads and universality—these things were a betrayal of reality, of Truth.

I get it; I do.

Was reality a series of people-pleasing, mixed messages? I loved that U2 concert era when they flashed *Everything You Know Is Wrong* across the big screens. I loved when *Believe* melded into *Lie* on the video monitors above. It *seemed* profound, but, um, was it?

What did we *know* that was wrong?

What dichotomy were they alluding to with that *believe* and *lie* thing?

Basically, I *did* approach U2 like one might approach a lengthy and committed marriage. I was in it for the long haul, and that big lemon on the PopMart Tour wasn't going to get in my way. But it occurred to me by the time I hit my thirties that I wasn't married to U2. I could give them and their lack of profundity up.

Standing in line for some kind of second wristband, Ann—arms crossed, contemplative, and poised—said, "I've come to realize something. When in doubt, wear the Doc Martens."

Very profound.

We were profound girls.

And soon after, we (of course) entered the heart in search of *Truth* with a capital "T."

And, well, then it's all very anticlimactic. We positioned ourselves on the Edge's side. As we strategically shimmied as close to the stage as possible, I whispered, "We're going to be marginalized."

Ann looked at me and replied, "No. We're going to be *marginalizing*."

Because, even though this was our big Divorce Gala, we wanted good seats.

Anticlimactic part: *It was a great show.*

I was so close that I could've touched Bono's toes.

Promptly afterwards, I pretended to give them up.

* * *

But that's not the end of the story!

So I ended breaking up with Ann instead, and not U2!

I didn't go out of my way to "choose" Bono; it just happened.

What if I told you that it turns out that this is a story about art and politics and religion?

What if I told you that I find my earlier dogmatism embarrassing and that I still think U2 has issues—but, damn it, I love them? And I believe that they're gifts to the world? And *their* issues are *my* issues?

And I love that epic grandiosity mixed with visions of world peace!

On September 19, 2017 (sixteen years after I gave them up that one time), U2 would come to town for the thirtieth anniversary tour of 1987's *The Joshua Tree*. By now, I was forty-seven, still married to the guy I fled the church with, the mother of two girls who knew all of the lyrics to "With or Without You," a breast cancer "survivor" (I don't love that word in this context), a part-time college prof, and the author of two books.

My relationship with Ann was naught.

Still a Christian, maybe less rigid. Perhaps, um, more generous?

What are the consequences of my cult days?

I'll say this and I'll say it once. This is for my church friends, the good Christian people, who wonder about Tim and me: We are phobic, scarred, insular. We don't want the church too close to our lives *ever again*. It was bondage. We have open wounds, so we're skittish in church socials, anxious when it's time to stand and greet your neighbor. I'm saying "we," but maybe I shouldn't: *I*.

I want to be on the outskirts.

Also, well, I had to redefine myself—and my relationship with U2.

For it was a relationship.

It's so silly to say.

Now, I was all full-fledged struggling (penniless) writer.

I was married to the kind of Christian who got thrown out of churches!

And Bono was like my brother I never met....

Somewhere along the line, I began to feel downright familial about Bono. Weird.

Especially since it's one-sided.

I even thanked him in the Acknowledgments of my first book.

Now, enmeshed in my sense of what it meant to be an Artist and a Christian, I looked at Bono (more than I looked at U2 as a whole) as a fellow Christian who was also an Artist (not a *Christian Artist*, but a *Christian who was an Artist*), and I saw a human struggling humanly with artistry and theology and popularity and disapproval. As silly as it sounded, I got it!

What did it actually mean to be a Christian and an Artist?

Who was my audience?

How does one effectively speak out against injustice?

How could I?

As it turned out, I was older—and somehow less enamored but rather empathetic with the plight of a band who sang songs like "Sunday Bloody Sunday," even if they also sang "Gone."

(I related to "Gone.")

Who am I to empathize with Bono? To feel kinship?

But I did!

* * *

In 2017, I wanted to pass the U2 torch to my kids.

Again, I declared my "retirement." This time, it had very little to do with the band. I just couldn't do that stadium thing anymore: the cacophony, the ringing ears, the standing—combined with my post-cancer/post-chemo incessant hot-flashing which would intensify in crowds, my exhaustion after nine-thirty at night, and my anxiety about going out without my husband who really had no desire whatsoever to see U2 (once was enough for him in the early 2000s).

I'd go to this one with my kids and my OG concert partner, Laura! For me, this was all about my girls, about artistry and politics and Christianity, about falling short but reaching high, about Laura.

On September 19, 2017, I'd retire (again)—but I wanted to be there with my kids to celebrate.

* * *

In 1987, Laura and I went to Paradise Valley Mall (closed) at the crack of dawn and waited in a real, physical line outside of a Dillard's department store. There was no Ticketmaster. Pearl Jam had not yet fought its losing battle against the concert ticket monopoly. But know this and know it well: *Eddie Vedder was probably doing the same thing in Seattle as we were in Phoenix, waiting in line for U2 tickets.*

Laura and I were not in line for tickets, actually. We were in line for *line tickets*, tickets to tell us how to get back in line. Once given a number, we were all rather polite and orderly. Then, at the given hour (9 a.m.?), we marched through—still in line—back hallways and a stairway to the box office counter and spent, like, twelve bucks each. First U2 concert.

Laura was my childhood. We moved from L. Frank Baum books to boys, from college to motherhood. And it was fitting that she was there for this other kind of closure. I wrote this passage for a blog called *Dear Teen Me* when my first book came out (I wrote it in 2012 and it's now gone off the web entirely*):

> Let's begin with a few startling revelations: Nick Rhodes will get a divorce, George Michael is gay, and Boy George is just bad news. You might as well wean yourself off of Mel Gibson right now, because he will not age well. And poor Patrick Swayze will die young, very young. Rick Springfield will have some brushes with the law: assault? DUI? You won't really care. Harrison Ford will still be cool, even though he pierced his ear and you always thought that was kinda silly, and he'll end up married to a woman only a few years older than you. Her name will be Calista. There's going to come this time when names like that will make you swoon; you'll forget pretty boys, and you'll be mesmerized by language and

---

*The one-time blog might have morphed into the 2012 book, *Dear Teen Me: Authors Write Letters to Their Teen Selves (True Stories)*; however, I've never read this book myself.

words and prose. Rather than being lulled into sleep by images of Duran Duran or Han Solo, you'll find yourself repeating sounds over and over: *Calista Calista Calista.*

Who had survived that era? Who was still with me in 2017?

There's that line in "The Fly" that I think Bono wrote, though it almost sounds like Andy Warhol: "Every Artist is a Cannibal."

I guess I do find the blatant self-aggrandizement of Bono, coupled with instances of apology and public humiliation and lyrics penned about one's own hypocrisy, to be, well, endearing.

Artistic.

What artists do.

A good artist is a cannibal.

But maybe that is not the right connotation. A good artist does not feed on others, but a good artist eats him- or herself alive. For the sake of art, for the sake of Truth, Beauty, and Goodness.

We feed.

I feed.

Perhaps, it is the cannibalism of U2 that appeals to me, the willingness to stand up for what's right and the willingness to look like an idiot and the willingness to expose foibles and the willingness to say, "I'm really good at this, and I do it for you."

That's it. Allow me to say it one more time: *It is the cannibalism, the willingness to stand up for what's right, the willingness to look like an idiot, the willingness to expose foibles, and the willingness to say, "I'm really good at this, and I do it for you."*

My favorite U2 song of all time is "Bad."

It's brash, bold, passionate, in-your-face, religious, cocky, political, existential, melodramatic, the most over-used descriptive word ever—"edgy," profound, subtle, about now, about the future, about America, about the planet, so sad, so silly, so right, about redemption, about hopelessness, about grace, minimalist, maximalist, naked, shameless, shameful, intimate, exaggerated, fictional, true, elusive, illustrative, compassionate, self-condemning, self-righteous, self-indulgent, full of self, about selflessness, too much in every way, Dr. Seuss meets the Devil, naïve, sexy, ugly, vulgar, lovely.

Has there ever been another rock 'n' roll song more lyrically beautiful?

Has there ever been a rock band more in touch with what it means to be human?

Kids Without Horses

Is that Art for you?
We went to the concert . . . .
Just the girls!
Tim stayed home.
I heard that Ann wasn't there. I don't remember who told me.
My kids knew every song.
We were on the floor (of course).
It was a new ceremony, a new rite, a new era.
Laura and I posed for pictures.
I passed the torch to my daughters.
They took it.
They took it and held it high.

The Vag Soliloquy: A New York Love Story

I've officially been writing this piece for about two decades. It pops up on miscellaneous occasions in my life and I mess with it, and then I push it aside—not for any particularly good reason. This, right here, will now be the official version.

This is my last New York Story. It's a love story.

When I lived in Manhattan for three and a half years in the nineties, I would occasionally write in the Winter Garden in the World Financial Center. I would sit at a table inside the enclosed space, scribbling away. I don't think whatever I wrote there ever turned into anything, but I remember the act of sipping my coffee, looking off the edge of the island, the roof above me made of glass. It was beautiful in the Winter Garden.

There were two TKTS spots in Manhattan to buy discounted Broadway tickets. One was in Times Square, right in the middle of everything, and the other was in the World Trade Center at the tip of Manhattan, one building away from the Winter Garden. Every time a friend visited me in New York, we would get cheap theater tickets at the TKTS box office, and I'd always go to the World Trade Center because there never seemed to be crazy lines and we could see the Statue of Liberty from within the Garden.

Somehow or other, I had managed to attend many unbelievable Broadway shows in the nineties like *Once on This Island* and *Miss Saigon*. There was *Bring in 'Da Noise, Bring in 'Da Funk* and *Rent*. *Crazy for You*. *Sunset Boulevard*. Discount tickets seemed doable back then. We'd sit anywhere, and every seat seemed good, and I have vague memories of people saying how Rudy Guiliani had really cleaned up Time Square. No one knew what was in store for Guiliani back then, and I had only heard a little about Mario Cuomo this or George Pataki that—very little sticks in my mind.

Kids Without Horses

My New York was the New York of a ghost/occupier. I was a squatter. I had taken my angsty, college-grad, impoverished-but-privileged, bedraggled-by-twenty, Tori Amos-loving butt into Greenwich Village (of course Greenwich Village), looking like an occupying country destined to eventually leave, either by force or truce. I was there for the short haul, not the long haul; my Times Square was just my Times Square—in the center of it all, lit up and frantic, a mid-nineties centerpiece in my young adult drama.

I was young.

Tickets were cheap.

My story, uncomplicated.

* * *

The last time I bought tickets at the TKTS box office was on August 10, 2001. I had left the City almost five years earlier. That trip to Manhattan in 2001 was my homecoming of sorts. I hadn't been back since I left on Christmas Eve 1996 in a huff, having thoroughly worn out my welcome.

A truce undoubtedly forced me out.

On Christmas Eve 1996, I taped up boxes for shipping (naked, I believe), said goodbye to favorite places (miscellaneous Village cafés), and closed my bank account (a shockingly simple affair). I fled by cab, which was a big deal because I was always broke and couldn't afford a taxi. But I splurged, opting out of dragging my belongings to Grand Central Station via subway where I'd catch a shuttle to Newark, all the time fearful I'd drop my laptop (which I had done the previous year). I didn't want to talk to the cabbie—I'm quiet with cabbies, silent with hairdressers.

As we drove away that Christmas Eve, I watched full-of-sorrows Manhattan blur in dull grays through dirty glass. I thought about another cabbie I once had on another splurge (he was probably a doctor or physicist in Sri Lanka) who had asked me to recommend one book for him—just *one*.

Like a great big cliché, I had said, *"The Catcher in the Rye."*

Leaving Manhattan in 1996—feeling like a New York failure—I was tempted to open up the window to shout obscenities like Holden did when he left Pencey Prep: "Good night, ya morons!"

I abstained, not wanting to make a scene.

Please know this: *It was me, not Manhattan.*

I love Manhattan.

I love New York.

But it had conquered me; I had not conquered it. I had wanted New York to be something it could never be for me. I thought it could be *Sesame Street*. I thought I'd get to know Oscar the Grouch and Big Bird. I pictured stoops and brownstones. Mr. Hooper. Hopscotch with interracial children. Sign language. Buffy St. Marie playing folk music.

When I came to grips with this impossibility, I altered my fantasy.

How about a Spike Lee film? Bed-Stuy? Me!

No?

An Artist in the Village?

Yes!

I'd be an Artist!

Still no?

Was I not chic enough? Okay, so I couldn't hustle and slither through the cool parts of town. The East Village knew I didn't belong right away. I lacked the languor, the ease, the unflappability. The West Village—sensing, undoubtedly, my poverty, my inner-dorkiness, and my puritanical heterosexuality—relegated me to a basement apartment, which I loved dearly, but I unquestionably always existed on the margins of the New York I wanted.

I was destined for basements.

Yeah, New York wasn't going to work after all.

So I left town on Christmas Eve 1996.

To soften the blow of leaving my favorite city in the world, I decided to go be a writer.

Crazy girl.

* * *

In August 2001, I arrived at Penn Station.

I was the visitor now.

Years had passed. I now lived back in Arizona. There had been tragedies, transformations. I was now over thirty. Still young, but old, too.

When I stepped out of Penn Station, I hadn't remembered the hot, muggy, smelly subway stations and the people pushing to climb the stairs to get out. On the street, I watched everyone going somewhere, no one idling. I saw their faces—those blanched, blank faces that were privileges. Those faces knew New York; they were proud of the drudgery. These were the faces of the bored and the chic, the exhausted and the hip. I remember trying to blend in with them, wanting to be bored and chic, exhausted and hip.

Kids Without Horses

I stayed with an old friend who had successfully acclimated. Rory, a Wall Street-type, lived in a Midtown high-rise. How had she done it, and why hadn't I?

Maybe she wasn't trying so hard.

New York in August 2001.

I spent my vacation days retracing old steps, forging once-familiar paths.

I went first to Taylor's Bakery in Chelsea (since closed). The whole-wheat rolls were still eighty-five cents but now it seemed like they were too big to eat in one sitting. Ethan Hawke, who had made SEVERAL neighborhood appearances in the nineties, didn't show. (I wanted to know, *Where the hell is Ethan Hawke?!?*) This was a big bummer, because I had wanted to pretend not to stare at him. Sitting on a bench across from the Chelsea post office, I almost cried. I thought of friends who had abandoned Manhattan before I did. Many of us had decided, together and separately, to be adults in other places. And that's where we were: *in other places*.

I could taste my forgotten world in the giant whole-wheat roll. In the flour, the flavor of the Manhattan landscape, unseen like a reptile's underbelly, touched my tongue: cafés on Bleecker and bars on Hudson, New England road trips and West Village side streets. Laundry Boys on West Fourth was now The Stinky Sock. The A&P on Sixth was now a Food Emporium. SPY Bar and the Bowery Bar, former hotspots, had closed. Art Greenwich or Greenwich Art movie theater (where I had seen many-a Winona Ryder film): *Vanished*. I walked past my old apartment in the Village and knocked on my landlords' door. They were spending a year in Provence. No one was home.

I trekked on, dripping with sweat. Café Mona Lisa for bowls of latte, Yaffa Café for fresh fruit. I wandered through the Village. I worried about West Nile Virus in Central Park because my mother had warned me.

I went to see *Ghost World* alone at the Angelika. I've only seen movies alone in Manhattan; I reserve that kind of loneliness for Big City environs. There, it feels somehow sanctifying, like a test of character. My first solitary film was *Hoop Dreams*, and I wept throughout the film. When I told my friend about it, she had said, "Only you would pick a three-hour documentary on basketball." But I remember those solitary movies. How I would open up a book before the previews began, hoping no one would see me buried in my novel. How I would muster up the courage to see romantic comedies featuring virtuous bad boys and supermodels who always knew just what to say. How I would plan the day around this brave and shameful act.

That August 2001, I spent my money on cappuccino, movies, and used CDs too.

Worried about the disappearance of my past, I bought Van Morrison, Cat Stevens, Patti Smith.

Patti Smith especially haunted my days.

* * *

Then, TKTS.

Rory worked at the World Financial Center, so I'd get us Broadway tickets and then maybe meet her for coffee at the Winter Garden.

I was buying tickets to see *The Vagina Monologues*, and I was embarrassed to say it aloud. I had really wanted to see this other play because Magnum P.I. was starring in it—but no one else cared. I guess that everyone else in line to buy tickets felt completely comfortable telling the TKTS guy, "*Vagina*! I want *Vagina*!"

I needed $134.00 for three tickets. Rory's sister who was one of my best friends was joining us, and I had $130.00 on me. They didn't take credit.

I frantically used my cell phone—the walkie-talkie kind—to call Rory next door at work.

No one answered. "Rory, it's me," I left a message after the beep. "I'm in line downstairs and I'm four dollars short. Can you come here *now*?" I didn't want to say that word, *vagina*. "They have the play we want to see."

And my phone promptly died.

I got to the front of the line. "Hi." I was sweating. "You're not going to believe this—I'm short four bucks."

A balding, middle-aged, Black guy looked at me from out of the box office window. "Which play do you want?"

I guess I had to say it.

"*The Vagina Monologues*," I whispered, leaning in close.

He didn't even blink.

"How many tickets?" He watched me carefully.

"Three." I scrambled to pull out money, my hands quaking. I looked pretty messed up, money flying everywhere. "I need three tickets. Just three."

I was trembling. I was shaking. I was thinking, *Please don't make me say* vagina *again*.

He put his hands through the window towards me, as if he were patting the air. With a calm voice, he said, "Okay, okay." He paused. "Take it easy."

I took a deep breath.

He took a deep breath. "How much do you have?"

I shuffled bills, counting them again. "One-hundred and thirty dollars—and," I held up a token for him to see, "a subway token."

He took another deep breath.

He made a *gimme* hand-gesture, took my $130.00 and the subway token, and handed over three tickets for *The Vagina Monologues*.

Yes, he did!

Do not believe what you hear about New Yorkers being rude.

* * *

Rory met me in the Winter Garden of the World Financial Center after my purchase. I had the tickets. People ate lunch at tables, looking out at the water. Some shopped. An Orthodox Jewish family ran a photo store by the stairs. I once saw a free Martha Graham ballet inside its marble space. Rory had to work, so I didn't stay long.

When I left Rory there that day, I left the Winter Garden forever.

Prior to leaving New York City in August 2001, I bought Rory a T-shirt that would most definitely offend many, many people I know. A thank-you-for-letting-me-sleep-on-your-couch gift.

The shirt said, *Fuck You, You Fucking Fuck.*

Rory loved it, as I knew she would.

She brought it to work to show her friends; she left it there in her desk drawer. That shirt was still there when the Towers went down about a month later. It was part of the ruins, never to be recovered.

The World Trade Center dissolved into ash on September 11. I watched it on TV from Phoenix. Rory survived. She remembers wandering Lower Manhattan in disbelief. I think she saw people jump from windows to their death before a plane hit. I never asked her if she had friends who died.

This is my small consolation: that TKTS man is probably still alive because the box office didn't open till late morning on September 11, 2001. (I looked it up in 2019, and they suffered no casualties.)

Love Rescue Me

It was closed when the Towers went down.

* * *

When I think back on my Gotham days in the nineties, I remember bands in small clubs, friends who left for other lives, the way it felt to walk on city sidewalks after midnight poetry slams, after sudden snowstorms, after foreign films at the Angelika. I remember the writing—all the writing. These hints of the person I would actually become, a kind of ephemerality to my days.

And that's what I remember most about New York City: the writing, the stories. The types, the shadows.

Much of that life crumbled or disappeared. Unanticipated parts were the lasting parts.

Not my unbelievable playbill collection.

Not my urban space with its solace.

Not the nineties with Ethan and Winona and Tori.

I had this image of how I wanted life to be. All *Sesame*, all Spike Lee.

I took another route, one without stoops in front of brownstones. That New York is gone for me.

But it's the place of my unearthing, the home of my unburying. Even though I didn't grow up there, I did grow up there.

My soliloquy. The Vag Soliloquy.

An ode to the writing life, planted in a winter garden.

Holy Ground (2020)

This came out in a Brooklyn literary journal (Vol. 1 Brooklyn) during the spring of 2020 after the Coronavirus was in full-swing. It would be my last published piece before the world seemed to stop. I had a new memoir out—my first book of nonfiction—whose book life might've been stymied by history. In this piece, though, I wanted to write about many things at once: my family's Thanksgiving 2019 road trip, my love of travel, how cancer had inundated all of my itineraries, the impact that another writer (Leslie Jamison) had on my writing, and my own mixed feelings about the ethics of tourism (is it okay to gaze upon "the ghetto"?) . . . .

Ba-Da-Bing

This is a discussion about road trips.

    In June 2015, I was diagnosed with breast cancer. Surgery, chemo, radiation, reconstruction, and more surgery followed. I'm hesitant to give away too much information, because I wrote a book about it—but this is my memoir's original title, so maybe you'll guess what I'm not really saying right now: *Cancer, I'll Give You One Year: A Non-Informative Guide to Breast Cancer* or *How to Get Your Ba-Da-Bing Boobies on the House!*

    In securing a pub deal (yay!), I dropped the *Ba-Da-Bing* part, and added *A Writer's Memoir, In Almost Real Time*. This was a fair trade, because I really wrote this book for three groups of people (not in this order): women, writers, and my kids. The first line is this: *This is a book about writing.*

Unraveling

People ask how cancer has changed my life. Am I more religious? Have I forsaken sugar? Do I still eat red meat? What's with the sex?

It's *in the book*, but:

1. I'm an introvert now.
2. I savor road trips.

The road trip part first: I've always loved travel. But now, I crave the jammed-in-the-car/free-hotel-breakfast/seven-hour-stretches-of-highway parts of a trip. I want to craft memories for my children. I want to unravel maps with them, holding their hands in White Sands or before a Renoir. I know life is a privilege.

But introversion is new to me. I've always been fairly extroverted, pretty social even. I *have* friends, *good* ones.

Cancer has rendered me insular. There are medical reasons, like exhaustion. However, there are other, ambiguous ones: I just want to be with Tim, my husband. (How crazy is this?) I'm a little nervous to be *out there* without him. I do it sometimes, venture into the world alone. I do writer things. I flew to Portland for a conference, went to Kentucky for a teaching gig, even. But it wasn't easy, and I craved my small world—though, like a mom cut loose temporarily, I luxuriated in the alone time. Still, I craved home, family, pets.

(Do you know, incidentally, how many times Tim has heard me read from my novel, *And So We Die, Having First Slept*? Like, a gazillion. *Because he's had to go with me to every single reading.*)

So, yes, I rarely go out past dark without him. Cancer has left me stumbling at dusk, longing for old marriage, a cat, Tim and his nightly bowl of cereal.

Cancer demanded of me that I get my house in order—because I was going to spend a lot of time in it.

Is this an essay on marriage?

No.

It's an essay on writing under the cancer rubric.

It's an essay on road trips.

It's an essay on writing about road trips under the cancer rubric.

Slum Tourism

Perhaps it's a good idea to ground ourselves in a loose theoretical paradigm.

Slum Tourism is treating poverty like a peep show. Have you heard of this before?

I looked it up—starting, of course, with Wikipedia (academic slummin'?).

In the nineties, I toured Harlem. Sounds awful in retrospect, but how else would I have seen the Abyssinian Baptist Church or the Apollo Theater back then?

I was with a mostly white student group, though our group included a beautiful Black girl from Texas. All together, we stood on a corner, in the supposed ghetto, a landscape of elegant brownstones, cracked pavement, and weathered storefronts.

Someone drove by and shouted, "Oreo!"

It took me a minute. To whom were they speaking?

Nicole. Our friend, a woman, African-American, Texan.

Nicole was so Jackie O (she probably wore a pillbox hat and carried a little purse).

My first slummin' memory.

I guess I've gone slummin' before then.

I guess it's part of my history.

Leslie Jamison

I never do hardcore academic work. But I love Leslie Jamison.

And she has informed my thinking on slummin' and tourism. I first read her nonfiction during the cancer fun. *The Empathy Exams* came out in 2014, but I picked it up in 2015.

I associate that book with my early bouts of cancer reclusion.

First, think back. Remember being a kid before the TV on a Saturday morning rife with Sugar Smacks cereal (the frog?) and "Speed Buggy" (did you know it was one season only?), and seeing on the screen a toddler in Ethiopia, naked, belly bloated, flies buzzing around lips, and some organization like the Global Famine Relief or Save the World Now announcing, *End Hunger Today?*

You'd stare.

You'd see it, and then wait for *Scooby-Doo* or *Shazam* to resume.

Love Rescue Me

Childhood in the seventies, eighties.

Poverty porn: exploitation to illicit a response.

Just another part of this slum tourism business: *voyeurism* and *otherness* mark them.

In *The Empathy Exams* and *Make It Scream, Make it Burn*, Jamison subverts this voyeurism of yesteryear by writing empathetically about different worlds, maybe misunderstood or unknown worlds. She speaks to people who genuinely believe their children are reincarnated war heroes. She talks to individuals, overwrought moms or undiscovered musicians or grownups with lousy childhoods, who have Second Lives in virtual reality, living as avatars. She talks with those who suffer from mysterious and possibly (not) phantom diseases. She explores the cacophony and garishness of Vegas; she thinks *deeply* about the life of a stepmom—because she was a stepmom.

Hers was my first text on cancer. The exploration of unknown lives.

It was a book on writing, too. *Doesn't she do what writers long to do? To go uninvited into worlds and make them their own, if only for a moment?*

Besides Jamison, I've given some thought to things that have impacted my own voyeuristic gaze. Undoubtedly, hipsters (and gentrification?) are important.

Maybe—just maybe—they've transformed slum tourism!

Consider the hipster. With those unkempt beards, Goodwill threads, Holden Caulfield caps or fedoras, they've become chic squatters, perhaps? (Do I envy them their squatting?) Taking their knitting, their urban beekeeping, their taxidermy (so I've heard!), their fine coffee, and their complicated vegan diets, they might've made slummin' *obsolete*. They've moved into the cool neighborhoods. They've colonized slums?

The world is now OUR slum.

Thank you, hipsters!

(The connection with gentrification may require too much brainpower for me. But we could go there.)

Slum Tourism, with a dash of Leslie and a splash of hipster—along with a daily dose of tamoxifen—paved my own Route 66.

Absurdity Tourism?

Route 66 calls me, and I've stood on a corner in Winslow, Arizona, not once but twice. (My kids say, "Too many times.")

I'm dying to go to that Tiny House Hotel in Portland. It pains me that I never went to Bedrock before it closed.

So let's forsake slummin' and think about hitting the road in search of humanity—absurd humanity, unruly humanity, solemn humanity, failing humanity, beautiful humanity, changing humanity, questionable humanity. Humanity that gets cancer.

The Scientology Building on Hollywood Boulevard! (*Free Shelly Miscavige.*)

All of Amarillo, Texas! (*We had a great time in Amarillo. Please visit Jack Sisemore's Traveland RV Museum.*)

Once, I visited Coney Island in search of two-headed babies; I think I saw a mermaid.

My personal coup d'etat, however, was Los Pollos Hermanos in Albuquerque, the chicken place in *Breaking Bad*.

Thanksgiving 2019

Destination: Inola, Oklahoma.

I love Tim's family. After fifteen years of marriage, they're my family, too. I mean it. *I really love them.*

But *Oklahoma*? Couldn't we meet in Boston? (The rest of the family is in Massachusetts.)

We leave in the Honda early one morning. Tim immediately puts on Christmas music, apparently trying to send me into anaphylactic shock.

The girls (ages twelve and thirteen) act like they hate each other 80% of the time these days, but on road trips, they play elaborate games of Dumbo and Lady (from *Lady and the Tramp*). Those stuffed animals were the best toy purchase ever made (Disneyland 2013). They will survive into the next decade, whereas the "My Little Pony" paraphernalia has been forgotten.

We pass abandoned, dying towns. Miami, Arizona. Beautiful in contemporary decline. A relic. Seymour, Texas. Desolation. How are communities abandoned? What happens that sends people packing?

Every time I see America, I think about how *The Walking Dead* missed so many opportunities for filming on location.

Every time I see America, I think about living without beauty. To dwell in unbeautiful parts. Dead parts. Dry parts.

I wonder at my choices. My desire for hustle, sprawl, frenetic clash and dazzle. I wonder, *Did I make this choice, or was I just born into it?*

We trail after Billy the Kid in Old Mesilla. We make footprints in New Mexico's White Sands. We balk at aliens in Roswell. Sweet Roswell.

At each stop, Tim and I are Indiana-Jones-in-Search-of-Coffee-and-Eccentricity. Show us a statue of Buddy Holly's glasses. Let's eat lobster bisque in Lubbock. Get us some coffee.

We spend three nights in Oklahoma.

I have lots to say about our semi-regular visits. I seem to unintentionally come off as this sharp-tongued City Slicker who has no clue how to walk through a dirt yard.

I know that, once, my Boston-born father-in-law and I exchanged "a look" when we couldn't find a coffee place within, like, a three-mile radius.

I know that, once, I put my foot in my mouth when I declared that *Touched by an Angel* was the dumbest show I'd ever seen on TV.

However, the real division is present, but mostly undiscussed: my husband's own North and South. We are the Protestants. They are the Catholics. Franciscans, even! They are Irish boys, these two brothers. A Sinn Fein/IRA ceasefire, implicitly in place. They don't argue religion. They don't even want to!

This has always struck me, because, well, there'd be arguing about religion on my side of the family.

Who are these people?

Why are they so nonconfrontational?

But underlying rigidities exist. Is it a Catholic/Protestant thing? A rural/urban difference?

The Franciscan contingent keeps pets outside, and Tim tries to convince me of the sheer joy a dog has running in the woods, tail flying in the wind. I remain unconvinced: dog on couch!

Their neighbor's daughter recently joined a cloistered convent. She's sixteen and she'll be a nun. Cloistered, she doesn't leave the convent. *Ever.* Even to get food. (Apparently, there's another nun who does the shopping for them.) There's a partition between her and visitors. Her life is supposed to be wholly devoted to prayer. I mean, she could leave if she wanted. But there she is, at sixteen. I am simultaneously awed at such conviction and enraged, holding back an outcry, my self-righteousness coupled with righteous indignation, too. This child! This girl!

However, Catholics and Protestants fully unite over Mr. Rogers' saintliness.

Kids Without Horses

We see the movie on Thanksgiving day. (Half of us see *Frozen 2*, and half choose *A Beautiful Day in the Neighborhood*.) I choose Mr. Rogers.

My sister-in-law asks me on the following morning, "Are you still thinking about Mr. Rogers?"

And I am! "Totally!"

(*He was a Protestant*, I resist adding.)

We share our Mr. Rogers' lessons: how attentive he was to the individual moment, how deliberately he lived. Did you notice how Mr. Rogers did not get distracted? How he gave each moment everything he had?

Mr. Rogers unites us in Inola.

We also go to an art museum; Tim says this is for me. They are generous, showing me art.

And my niece is tall, lovely, an Okie, also sixteen like the neighbor-nun. She spouts admiration for Kanye West's conversion (which I pooh-pooh). She says, "I'm very passionate about this." She sings the Chick-fil-A song from *Jesus Is King*. She delivers political riffs, telling us about her MAGA hat. *I hold my breath.* Later, Tim, touching my shirt, whispers, "You're all sweaty from talk of Trump."

In truth, she reminds me of me at sixteen, but I had a different Kanye and a different hat.

But I think about my own children, too, and I deliver tirades telepathically: Girls, we love your cousin, lithe, Catholic, fervent, faithful. But *you* are not cloistered, and *you* will not be cloistered, and *you* have seen this America that they say needs to be made great again, and greatness has more to do with Native American ruins in Old New Mexico and that bakery we ate churros at in Roswell and bony horses in impoverished Texas. It even has more to do with alien crash landings and Chick-fil-A. America is this hashtagged landscape, this broken territory of rundown gas stations and displaced people and the Bob Dylan art we saw next to the Dorothea Lange photos of the Great Depression in Tulsa, of all places.

I practically shout, *We are not cloistered!*

On road trips, I often pontificate about America.

Going home, we visit the oldest zoo in the southwest (Alamogordo, New Mexico); we skip the Shroud of Turin Museum. We accidentally pass up Steins, a ghost town—a new forever regret.

I finally see *The Thing* off I-10. Overrated. (Look it up, seriously.)

We eat at Popeye's. Pretty good.

Our trip: voyeuristic, cancer-haunted, annotated and insular.

Ethics

Is this fixed gaze objectification, exploitation?

I remember my trip to Dachau in 1990. A former concentration camp in a quaint town near Munich. No bones, no ashes. Whitewashed, mere echo chambers.

Should we have gone inside, or should we have turned abruptly, refusing to see, never memorializing, maybe even razing that provincial town to the ground?

China in 1997. Robin took me as her "writer" when she launched Girls Global Education Fund. Really, I didn't do anything. Except steal stories for later.

But were those rice paddy-enmeshed villages dying? Would entire dilapidated villages disappear, like Venice, Italy, but without any fanfare? And what of my writerly wanderings? What of our Shanghai rushes to McDonald's, which we sought out like refugee centers, our comfort in the Big Mac announcing our U.S. citizenship? Where is the morality in my Guangzhou market strolls as I photographed hanging dead animals?

Soweto in 1997. Shantytowns. *Apartheid* ruins. *But you don't understand*, I'd insist. South Africa was my heart, soul, beginning, end. But what can I say about horseback-riding in Swellendam or wine-tasting in Stellenbosch? How do I explain those dips into luxury in the midst of decay? Dear Lord, was my participation in the braai a crime against humanity?

Cuba in 2004, a school trip, an education visa. No Cubans were allowed inside our Havana hotel, except for employees. Our rooms had CNN—but across the way, ramshackle apartments were lit up by TV screens without access to American cable news. One day, a tsunami or hurricane might wipe out the whole city. These buildings would be swept into the sea. Havana certainly awaited disaster. The Spanish teacher was cute, Mexican-American. One night, coming back from dinner, Lisa was stopped in the lobby when she was entering the hotel. They told her, *No Cubans allowed!* They apologized profusely, not meaning to mistake her for a whore.

The Jewish Cemetery in Prague, thirty years ago. A fairytale city with drawbridges, cobblestone, and swans (that bit!). The graveyard was *breathtaking*: dense, medieval, layered, disorderly. It reeked of meaning: *Life is for the living; death is for the dead.*

I remember thinking, *This is how to acknowledge the value of life.*

What does it mean to traipse through graves?

Is tourism deeply, deeply irreverent?

Road Trip

We are decidedly uncloistered.
 We celebrate eccentricity.
 Fondling the living, their artifacts.
 Gazing upon the world in aching adoration.
 We do not traipse over graves. Rather, we declare, *Your world is holy ground.*

An Essay About Cancer

We take epic road trips now.
 I'm introverted.
 What I mean is: I'm living on borrowed time.
 My time is borrowed.
 Sometimes I mention insomnia, my flesh on fire, my body ravaged.
 My body is the Jewish cemetery, a Chinese village.
 My body, a shantytown.
 I say to my children, *We are voyeurs.*
 I say to my children, *Girls, your world is holy ground.*
 Your world
 is
 holy
 ground:
 Holy, holy
 ground.

Nothing Sacred: Summer 2021

The working title of this Summer 2021 piece was "The Audacity of My Very Existence." We survived the summer of 2020, turning inward inward inward. In 2021, with some trepidation, we stepped out.

Andrew Cuomo as Metaphor, May 2021

This is also a discussion about road trips.

It is the summer of 2021, and the world has changed.

Yet here we are again.

It is summer, and we are vaccinated (there is a vaccine now). Biden is president, and I'm done with politics. The cop who killed George Floyd is in jail. My kids attended in-person school all year. Andrew Cuomo was a good guy, and now he is a bad one. Hong Kong is messed up, and Russia is Russia. Putin, still Putin. China, bad news. The border, our border, is not good. Really, I don't want to belittle any of it; I, am, however, exhausted. I expect Biden to compromise my convictions, but less so than Trump. Everything is horribly partisan these days, and I have stepped out.

I have settled back into my mom-self, hoping frankly, to relive the magic of last summer when we hunkered down—the four of us—sequestered, quarantined, our adventures limited but heighted.

I told you about the summer of 2020: It was all *Criminal Minds* and the Mogollon Rim which I had been pronouncing as "Mongolian Rim." It was the infamous Trump-memorabilia Trumped Store in Show Low and the best pulled pork sandwich of my life in Panguitch, Utah. It was Pinetop, Arizona, and Strawberry, Arizona, and an eight-mile-a-day walking quota. Oh, it was our summer of privatized family vacations; it was our summer of my highfalutin interpretations.

It's over now.

My kids are enflamed by the desire to run.

Kids Without Horses

They want to flee from the audacity of my very existence.

There's no going back to that old Andrew Cuomo. Once you know, you know.

Mostly, this is an essay about being done.

Bucket List, End of May 2021

I don't know. I mean, I'd *like* to get to England before I die. Before I'm *really* done.

Though I gave up rock 'n' roll concerts after U2 in 2017, I could be sweet-talked out of retirement.

I've reluctantly given up the tiny house idea. We went to a motor home show a few weeks ago in the same stadium where I got vaccinated and saw U2, and Tim and I scoped out the RVs as if the option were really on the table. We'd just seen *Nomadland*. That's why. *Blame it on Frances McDormand.*

Actually, though, I have to be honest with myself. It's unlikely I'd do a damn thing to help Tim with set-up at any RV site. And I think set-up involves sewage. Not to mention electricity or water or internet.

I love the idea of being on the road like some kind of beatnik—but *sewage?*

Hooking up things?

And are we talking about *Quartzsite*, in the bone-dry desert near Blythe, California?

Blythe, the rest stop between Phoenix and Disneyland?

Do you *know* Blythe?

If we get an RV, will we be excluded from the places I truly want to go, like the impossible streets of San Francisco? Could we drive that monster into Chicago, down Michigan Avenue? Would I be limited to, um, the *outskirts*?

Yeah, I guess I'd prefer a Hampton Inn with a crappy free breakfast. In a city.

So I add the West Fork Trail in Sedona to my 2021 bucket list, right around the time I drop the tiny house and RV fantasies (still knowing that I'd kinda like to go to that Jack White concert, but I probably won't).

I gotta hike the West Fork Trail.

Before I die.

At some point, post-cancer, my desire flared: I wanted to *walk on all the trails*. I'd give up tiny houses, but I'd be a trailblazer. Why this desire to trailblaze?

It's connected—fiercely—to *The Accident*, to cancer and, undoubtedly, it was aggravated by Covid. In other words, *my mortality*.

By hanging onto Tim, I can hike easy trails. I can try moderate trails. Is it some kind of desire for accomplishment or athleticism? An old fascination with the Yellow Brick Road? Do I want to make my way into an Enchanted Forest? Do I long for paths and journeys and trickling streams and *especially* Oz?

Urban, desert, forest: I'll take Sabino Canyon and the Pink Ledges. I can do Bisbee and Manhattan.

Let me hold onto Tim and hike through forest. Let him drag me up mountaintops, pull me through Aspen groves, get me to the Oregon Coast or the White Mountains.

Before. I. Die.

Much to my children's chagrin, Tim and I have put in the miles *and miles*, often with them in tow. For a crippled girl, I've covered *a lot* of terrain. I'm not joking. Alcatraz to Chinatown, the Chicago Bean and back, Redwood trees and the Oregon coast.

I like to see stuff.

And Tim does, too.

So, yeah, the West Fork Trail in Sedona!

Our first summer 2021 adventure.

The West Fork Trail becomes monolithic in my head.

I had seen pictures taken by my friend Odette, and it looked exotic under the red rocks of Sedona. "It's easy," Odette had said; she even took her old dad when he visited town. He's, like, ninety-something. A ninety-year-old man!

But I forget.

I forget that Odette's *Dutch*.

Everyone knows they're a *hardy* people.

I mean, Corrie Ten Boom.

I mean, Odette can kick *butt*.

So we do it, we hike the West Fork Trail—me, blind to the realities of Odette as a woman.

The trail is easy, I *guess*.

Except for the fifty trickling streams one must cross by *balancing* on *slippery* rocks and fallen tree trunks. I *guess* it's easy if one is adept at *hopping* from one *submerged* rock to another *submerged* rock like a Disney character. Especially if you're a baby deer or a talking squirrel in a skirt or, better, a rabbit.

Red rock formations hover all around on the West Fork Trail: we journey over an enflamed planet with creeks. And I always assume that the same guy who will hook up my sewage tank at Quartzsite will also get me across the rushing water.

I assume correctly.

Even though Odette's old dad from Holland still runs marathons and the West Fork Trail is nothing to him, and even though I spend the very bulk of my life in hot denial about the fact that I cannot cross rivers and balance on the edge of cliffs, I forge ahead.

Listen, my denial is thick.

Maybe I just want to *think* of myself as someone who treks. A vagabond. I have to live with the fact that I'll never have an Airstream or a tiny house, I'll never hike the Appalachian Trail (another weird fantasy), and it's even unlikely that I'll ever again sit on a train station floor in the middle of the night in a foreign country, miscellaneous small amounts of currency hidden in my sock, waiting for a train to take me somewhere, anywhere.

I know I'll never sit on a train station floor in a foreign country again.

The last time I sat on a train station floor in a foreign country, I did not appreciate the fact that I was sitting on a train station floor in a foreign country.

In our first adventure of the summer of 2021, how might I communicate to my disengaged girls on the West Fork Trail in Arizona that this is, indeed, their *Era of the Train Station Floor*?

Dear girls, I'm just hiking the easy trails now.

I Read Books, June 2021

First, John Steinbeck's *Travels With Charley*. In 1960, he took a road trip (with his standard poodle) to think about America. I want this for myself: my own journey across America. With my dog, Snickers.

Before. I. Die.

I have a friend who thinks democracy in America is experiencing its death throes, in light of the wild divide between political parties. I doubt he's right, but just in case America is done . . .

I've got some sightseeing to do.

I hike the West Fork Trail in Sedona, hanging onto Tim, channeling Odette, meditating on America. I am American. I am Frances McDormand. I am Corrie Ten Boom. I read Steinbeck.

Second, I read most of the books by the late Rachel Held Evans, for whom I feel immense affection. She passed away recently, too young, a Christian, a writer, and a mom. "A popular Christian author," people say. Rachel had an allergic reaction to a med, and her brain started to swell. She was thirty-seven.

I tend to revile Christian books despite my religiosity, but I decide to find out what I'm thumbing my nose at. My disdain has always been aimed at the sentimentality spiel, coupled with sexist ideas and entirely disingenuous pontifications. But, well, what the heck? I'd read Rachel!

It turns out I like reading her, knowing that this kind of woman was out there, *authentic*, fighting the good fight. I like knowing we disagreed theologically sometimes—but I could still *like* her, *really* like her. I read her, and I mourn.

Third, I read a book by Ethan Hawke.

My age. Old.

Ethan, my longtime friend.

When I'm not reading, I engage in more mom-life, which means that I drive places. I try to listen to my kids' music and I wonder about this trend of turning adolescents into stars. I feel nostalgic for the daggers of Stevie Nicks.

As I listen to their music, I wonder if angst and emotional terrorism and that mind-controlling preoccupation with relationships is for the young. Have my old faves "aged out" of passion? Is this why my kids can gleefully say to me, "Okay, Boomer."

To which I dutifully respond, "I'm Gen X."

I'm haunted by aging.

The *Before-I-Die*-ness of my life.

The Commitment, End of June to the Beginning of July 2021

We finally go on the big vacation to Massachusetts.

Within the last year or two, I make this commitment to Tim. I say: "I'll move wherever you want, if we can just stay in Phoenix till the kids graduate high school."

He takes me up on it!

I mean, why not? I've done some border-crossing, train-riding, right?

Granted, all of it happened before the turn of the century, before I find my true self on the couch with a pet, analyzing an Amazon Prime limited series starring Kate Winslet or Jason Bateman. My tru*er* calling. My *truest* calling.

I agree to move to Massachusetts for him. *Just let my kids graduate high school first.*

I knew he'd take me up on it.

When we discuss moving, I rule out some possibilities.

I rule out Oklahoma, where his bro is. Miscellaneous reasons having to do with cultural biases that make me inherently a lousy person.

Dallas, Texas might've been a work option for Tim, but I am, um, *unenthusiastic*. Texas interests me, voyeuristically (see slum tourism discussion elsewhere). Like I'm curious about Chip and Joanna and the Branch Davidians in Waco, Ted Cruz being all Ted Cruz, and that fierceness Texans seem to have—but, well, we all know it's not for me, dragging in my faux-New Yorker/moderate Arizona bod into real cowboy territory. Don't mess with Texas, *my ass*.

Tim isn't going for the Oregon coast. All the libs scare him, despite those perfect little coastal towns.

A victorious return to Greenwich Village ain't gonna happen. *Insert sad-face.*

San Francisco sounds like a good time, but we've all heard about the poop on the streets.

I like the idea of "trying out" the South, but I think Tim envisions me constantly embarrassing him with my Yankee-Antifa ways. (He's probably right. I'd likely make some comment about Confederates or inadvertently call someone *Bubba*.)

Florida has alligators, swamps, humidity.

But New England?

Boston?

His parents live in a charming little Massachusetts *hamlet*, which they probably do not refer to as a *hamlet*.

And suddenly I am committed to moving to Massachusetts in 2025!

We'll take the pets and my mother.

The Truth: *I owe it to him.*

Yes, I'll be damned if I didn't keep his shit together that first decade. I don't care what narrative he weaves.

But he had us for the last term.

And never forget other things: He's my sugar daddy, I lack all career ambition and call myself a "writer" despite my dismal publishing history, he's grown to like my cats—and there are *always* cats—though he only truly loves the dog, he's a good father despite the fact that he typically makes me out to be the bad guy, I pick 99 percent of our movies and TV programs, which might include a godawful zombie show, the only reason why I hike on a million trails is that he's dragging my sorry butt up and down mountains, he'd literally destroy any other woman to whom he was married (he denies this), I'd kill any other man to whom I was married (I do not deny this), he says I can take my mom with us to New England and that's no joke, pets are non-negotiable including multiple cats, and he's a good guy—like, seriously, ladies, how often can one honestly say, *He's a good guy*? We love each other. We're all *for better, for worse.* We work as a couple, though I look like hell and no one would ever believe that I was once semi-cute. Briefly, in the eighties.

So we go to Massachusetts in the summer of 2021, knowing, *foreshadowing,* a future move—when we're empty-nesters. A state of being that literally makes me curl up and die, just a little.

(This is apparently an essay on death, not road trips.)

Basically, on this vacation, a few important things happen:

I slam my thumb in my in-laws' screen door upon entering their house on the very first night (coming straight from the airport in Boston), but I can't tell anyone though it kills because I promised myself I wouldn't have any medical disasters there—having had others that landed me in the hospital in Leominster on previous trips. It takes about six months to fully heal. (I suffer covertly, and my thumbnail turns black.)

I eat two lobster rolls in Maine in one day without regret. I will often think fondly of those lobster rolls, especially the first. Which I ate while lounging on the beach with a breeze.

I offend the liberals with my conservativism and the conservatives with my liberalism. Seriously, I alienate Trumpsters by suggesting that they sold out their integrity, I support getting vaxxed, I look down on pot which I guess we all call *weed* now, and I scoff at the sexual mores of everyone. Like, *within a one-hour period.* I am so unequivocally uncool, it's shocking.

My confrontation-phobic kids are mortified and disgraced. Tim deals, but I'm fairly convinced I finally did it: *alienated his entire family*.

Tim and I get in a dumb fight at lunch (awful veggie burgers) in Indian Head in New Hampshire. We were vacationing away in New Hampshire, and now we're headed back to Massachusetts. We have a bunch of kids with us, so we're sitting alone at a table waiting for the very bad food while our extended family laughs it up a few feet away. *The fight is brutal, memorable, haunting, another one of our secrets.* He gets up and walks away from me. He comes back. Story of my life. It's a happy story. Do I believe this? *I do.* Why is this important? *Because we both remember it, like shame, like a permanent heart murmur.* Our love story is half cardiac arrest, half lobster roll on the sea.

And then, then, that very night, he tells me I'm the one he loves the most. We are at a restaurant for dinner with the entire family—who are now kinda suspicious of me—in Fitchburg, Massachusetts. I eat more lobster: a lobster pie. *I guess Tim can tell me any damn thing he wants. Walk away. Come back. Feed me lobster.* I obsess about how his family must regard me. They must be confused. Do they see me as strong? Their son's safety, their son's soulmate, their son's solace—or do they see one crazy, power-hungry, whip-and-chain bitch from hell? Anyway, *lobster pie.*

Tim and I find trails in the White Mountains that are AMAZING. So beautiful. *File away with lobster.*

My kids completely abandon us for their cousins. I barely see them.

I read a novel, also on the beach in Maine, about the Shah's Iran and the Islamic Revolution under Ayatollah Khomeini.

Someone asks Wendy if her parents always spend so much time together, to which she responds, *Yes.*

Yes, they do.

Fun Over, August 2021

And then it is over.

We plan for one day in Flagstaff on the thirty-first of July for my youngest daughter's fourteenth birthday. On the drive to Flagstaff, Tim plays me a playlist he made for our seventeenth anniversary, and I don't tell him that it's the most beautiful thing I've ever heard.

We walk through a magical pocket of Aspen trees, and it might be the most beautiful trail I've ever been on.

We drive to downtown Flagstaff and eat Thai, and it's probably the best Thai I've ever eaten.

After Flag, the adventures are over.

The Delta variant really grabs national attention, just in time for school to resume.

I know Trump still lurks, but I barely pay attention.

We decide to go vegan for a month, and we last for exactly four meals. It's the jackfruit that does us in. Jackfruit Tacos. The whole family just simultaneously folds. *No jackfruit.*

I also think, for sure, that I have asymptomatic Covid because I find that I don't like my coffee as much as I used to. What's up with that? It's gotta be Covid.

My friend Scott says, "Switch to a different brand of coffee."

We obsess over HBO's *Succession*, and act as if we've discovered pure gold.

Mostly, I lament uneasily.

Mostly, I feel loss quietly.

I mourn the end of our emotional quarantine, the way the events of 2020 played out as a poignant battle between Good and Evil. It had been us against the world. My babies had needed me. Going out for supplies had been my own apocalypse, a futuristic scavenger hunt. It was Tim and I, no matter what. The world was ugly and George Floyd was dead, but I had seen beauty in the midst of terror. I had seen murals in alleyways and forest paths and things were clearly right, clearly wrong.

This year demands more of me; this year demands less.

This year, I am wondering at what point do my kids love me again—or maybe it is simply over.

Will they love me *Before I Die*?

In the summer of 2021, I was audacious.

I burned crops.

I spared no feeling.

I was loveless, breastless, breathless, tacky, inappropriate, a helicopter mom.

A hag, a nag, a harpy.

As August edges its way into autumn, the rain soaks the ground.

Tonight, I look on the gray clouds, the obscured and dark sky, the wet earth.

I mourn the end of a season.

From holy ground, we traverse this place, this desert, where nothing is sacred.

An Untitled Poem

At first,
I wanted breaks.
I wanted one hour, maybe two—
alone at Starbucks, with my book.
I read a Marilynne Robinson novel,
Home,
and I held back tears when I got to the end,
and made weird gulping sounds
so as not to make a scene
in public.
The last page was so beautiful,
and I was
so fragile—
just wanting to be by myself for a moment
to escape your delicacy and need.
Over a decade later,
I want time
I want weekends, your commitments—
family vacations, just the four of us.
We'll drive off on highways in the minivan,
that vehicle of my demise.

Love Rescue Me

We'll walk through Aspen forests,

eat free hotel breakfasts.

Or we can stay home:

watch *The Office* together,

eat veggie burgers and sweet potato fries—

I'll find the cat, put her in your lap.

Just be with me—

let me see you there,

here, next to me, always.

IV

I Am Writing Blindly

This section is about writing.

If I were to list all of the works that have contributed to my writing life, I know that J.D. Salinger's The Catcher in the Rye *and an essay by Roger Rosenblatt called "I Am Writing Blindly," which appeared in* TIME *Magazine on Monday, November 6, 2000, would top the list.*

In August 2000, two explosions (mechanical failures) destroyed a Russian sub called the Kursk in the Barents Sea—water touching Norway and Russia. Inside the sub, 118 people died instantly. Twenty-three people survived for a few hours and found shelter inside the destroyed sub, realizing their fate and eventually succumbing (suffocation). Rescue attempts were marred by disaster and, ultimately, failure.

Rosenblatt, emotionally moved, wrote his TIME *essay about how these dying men, in their final hours, took it upon themselves to write. They wrote notes to loved ones.*

This is all natural, of course.

But Rosenblatt, in this example of artistic genius (you can see I love this essay, which is readily available online), renders the very act of writing to be existential, philosophical.

I've taken his zingers with me. I've digested them, played with them. I live by them.

I Am Writing Blindly

My own interpretations: Writing is proof that there is a God. Writing is metaphysical. Writing is an affirmation of meaning. By committing pen to paper, we commit to meaning. We can't help it. It's what we do.

To be crude:

Our sub is going down.

We are dying.

We write.

And we write.

And we write.

We must write.

Slaapstad: An Investigative Reporter at an International Rave at the End of the Century

In 1997 and 1998, I went to South Africa because (a) Nelson Mandela was the first democratically-elected president and Apartheid *was over, (b) I had an American friend there, and (c) I wasn't exactly pursuing "professional growth" in any traditional way.*

Fiction is my shroud: my truest true.

That's what I believed until I started writing nonfiction—in which you *curate* and *craft* the truth, right?

My first book was fiction. *The Freak Chronicles* was written on the run: expat fantasies. It was born in Cape Town.

It was *true*; it was a *lie*.

This might be my one and only nonfiction piece about South Africa. It's morbid.

I arrived in Cape Town in 1997 on the pretense of *being there,* of historicity. Nelson Mandela, *the* Nelson Mandela, free after twenty-seven years on Robben Island (the South African equivalent to Alcatraz—equally spooky, isolated, colorless), was the first post-*Apartheid* president of South Africa. I was *there for it. I was there.*

Despite my noble intentions, the stories I wrote were about Unhappy Women Abroad, The Lost Generation's children exploiting exchange rates, alcoholic missionaries. About girls losing their idealism and Afrikaners coping with their legacy of racism and domination. About morphing from New-Yorker-with-sizzling-CV to comatose girl with ambiguous relationships that ended, promptly, when she was rolled onto a plane in a wheelchair pushed by her mother. (Actually, I've never fully written that story—but you can *feel* it there, between the words.)

Yes, South Africa would end badly for me.

I Am Writing Blindly

* * *

Freak was the book I published after exile, after my tour bus rolled on June 1, 1998, after I was thrown out a window on my way to Namibia, landing by the side of a road, brains bashed in.

Brains literally bashed in.

I went to South Africa twice (in 1997 and in 1998); I stayed for a while when I went the second time, and the Verve's "Bittersweet Symphony" was popular at the time. I have distinct memories of walking poolside in the hostel in a suburb ironically named *Observatory*, at the age of twenty-eight, sun shining, a cadre of attractive foreigners sunbathing, and I was quietly singing along to the Verve: *"I'm a million different people/From one day to the next . . . ."* Having literally just quit my life in New York, where I had unambitiously been working on the fringes of international relations, I had decided to "be a writer." I'd get my MFA after my expat time.

That was the plan until I bashed my brains in.

But in Observatory, Cape Town, in those brief, pretend-adult moments, I lived like an investigative reporter at an international rave at the end of the century, and I discovered—much to my internationalist surprise—that I was *very* American. I barged into rooms like an American, and I assumed I was the Superpower on the premises. I couldn't even help it! Americans are bulls in china shops! I was one! Though my final trip ended in tragedy, returning home—still, shockingly, saying, *I'm going to be a writer*—those were some "American Abroad" Days!

Man, oh man.

I guess that *The Freak Chronicles* would be my fictional true equivalent to Mark Twain's *The Innocents Abroad* or *The New Pilgrim's Progress* (which I've never actually read, but I like saying this and drawing a connection between Twain and me).

I think I'm obsessed with the makings of a writer.

I mean, what was I doing?

I mean, why?

I mean, are you kidding me?

Or was I just an American girl demanding global attention?

* * *

When I was in South Africa, crazy things happened.

I saw U2 perform at Green Point Stadium on March 16, 1998.

Of course, U2.

Big sigh from my readers: *Why does everything have to be about U2?*

I don't know. It just does.

It was the first time they performed in Africa. I mean, *I was there AGAIN!* A happy accident!

Well, you gotta know something about what it takes to make up the kind of writer I would eventually become: one must possess a touch of nihilism, a smidgen of existential dread, a more potent dose of Christian orthodoxy; one should have a penchant for lousy relationships with bad boys who are also famously pretty boys which strikes people as odd because one is rather low on the totem pole of gorgeous women; one should be guilt-ladened by miscellaneous sins and other things like an *Americanness* which really shows up as if under some kind of UV black light in certain circumstances; one should be philosophical about foreign affairs and racism and the plight of humanity, in possession of a rather dry wit, biting tongue, and awkward social techniques. *One should be very, very awkward.*

Obviously, there will be future books *and* psychiatric bills.

"Every Artist Is A Cannibal" flashed on big U2 concert screens that March night.

(We've already discussed it, but allow for this obsessing.)

Every Artist Is A Cannibal.

I could feel the excitement, the artistry, the writerly impulse . . . .

Was I a cannibal? Do artists chew people up, spit them out? Do artists feed on pitfalls and weaknesses and dark human sagas? And me, worldly, decadent in my Americanness, sleepwalking through shantytowns: *Didn't Franz Kafka write about the Hunger Artist? Do we make art out of our own destruction? Would I, could I, eat myself alive for Art?*

Would I, at the end of the day, eat myself alive for Art?

Me, pontificating on U2 and Art! Old news . . . in an exotic setting.

I remember only two things about that concert (besides the flashing screens).

I attended with a German girl named Greta who lived in the same international youth hostel as I. She was stoic, beautiful, and so German. I disliked Greta and I think she disliked me, too, because she flirtatiously blew off the hot Afrikaner son who owned the hostel and who I was then dating. I was electrified by her confident lack of interest in him.

Electrified!

I Am Writing Blindly

What did she possess inside that allowed for her refusal, and why didn't I possess it?

Didn't her coolness towards the hot Afrikaner indict me for *not* blowing him off, as well?

Didn't her indifference towards the hot Afrikaner suggest that I was a *sellout*, despite my noble ideals and highfalutin talk about Nelson Mandela and Desmond Tutu?

Didn't her chill towards him say to me, *I am done with Nazism—what's your problem, weak American girl?*

I literally thought this stuff when I looked at her.

Can you say, CRAZY?

Nonetheless, Greta wanted to see U2, too.

After all, we were two world travelers, living it up.

Yay!

Greta and I had shared a hostel room for a while. Kids from Europe, kids from America. Backpacks, single beds. I'd roll over at 4 a.m. and see Greta, topless. It was a weird thing, indeed. She'd sleep naked (in a hostel) with the sheets down to her waist, breasts exposed.

Like, her breasts were *totally* exposed.

I'd think, *American girls don't do that, Greta.*

I'd think, *American girls don't expose ourselves while sleeping, leaving ourselves so vulnerable, so open for attack.*

I'd think, *Good Lord, brazen German girl! Cover up and stay the hell away from my boyfriend who grew up under* Apartheid!

I'd pause in the middle of the night, shocked, then defensive.

I'd think, *Greta, what the hell are we doing in this Godforsaken country with its insane past and racist scars? Greta, shouldn't you pull up that sheet and remember Hitler, and shouldn't I kiss this white boy goodbye, and shouldn't we head back to Western Civ?*

Greta, we gotta get out of here, girlfriend!

So Greta and I went to see U2 together. We were, after all, First Worlders.

United, I guess.

That was one thing I remember about the concert.

But I also remember Bono, looking out over the notably low-energy audience—who were unfamiliar with rock etiquette (South Africans really weren't accustomed to our global rock 'n' roll ways quite yet—the whole world had *just* stopped boycotting them). Bono looked out and called Cape Town *Slaapstad*.

"Sleepytown."

That's all I remember.

He called Cape Town "Sleepytown."

We were asleep.

* * *

I end suddenly.

In June 1998, my mother flew to Africa to retrieve me, her brain-injured daughter, who was, the woman discovered, involved in an international crime scene. Having a fling, expat-ing all over the place, not really changing the world or even writing all that much. My mother packed up her kid's nomadic belongings, booked flights to the States, and sought medical care. I'd spend the rest of June in a rehab hospital in Chicago. I'd never see Greta or the hot Afrikaner guy again. I think of Slaapstad often, and I don't really remember it as sleepy at all.

What to make of this medley of my indiscretions?

Artists as cannibals, *Sleepytown* metaphors, my comatose self, Nelson Mandela looming behind me when in front of me all I could see was that Afrikaner guy, so beautiful, who did not fill me with love but only a kind of sorrow upon reflection. How dare I fall prey to that? How dare I allow myself to be lulled into apathy by South African sunsets and braais on the beach? How dare I forsake my political rage? Had I traded in my do-gooder card for self-destructive artistry?

And could someone, *anyone*, tell Greta to cover up?

Greta, for God's Sake!

Alas, *The Freak Chronicles* was born in Slaapstad.

In South Africa, I was a million different people.

At once, political and apolitical.

At once, a piece of fiction and a piece of nonfiction.

Of course, I revert to fiction to tell the truth.

I will stick to my fiction.

A disguise, a covering, a shroud.

My Sweet Cannibalism.

Walter

I wrote this for a class on travel-writing (which I adore!), and it was published in a small journal during the summer that my dad died in a car accident (2002). I've rewritten it a few times. I've also tried and failed to look up the real Walter on Facebook. Oh, well.

Summer 1990

The Berlin Wall has come down. Gorbachev is still in power. Madonna posters adorn Helsinki. Iraq is on the verge of attacking Kuwait.

I am a kid, a college girl; my hair is a different shade of red. Some call it *Bozo orange*. I prefer *brassy, sun-drenched*. The snapshots of that summer are dusty and dated. Now, they have that pallor of rerun TV—they're nostalgic, sweet, a little sad.

Walter, Leningrad (June 1990)

Walter is in his early thirties, so he's old. We're part of a student group from my college on a five-week Russian language immersion summer program in the Soviet Union, and most of us, American kids, envision careers in embassies; little do we know that the Cold War is almost over.

But Walter is Canadian, and maybe he said he was a management professor at Harvard. Managing what, I don't know. He's from Harvard?

One day, all of us hanging out somewhere on Nevsky Prospect, he announced, "I'm not going to pretend we're keeping in touch, because we won't." Then, he looked at all of us, including the girl with whom he was having a fling, and added, "So don't write me."

That was back when we wrote letters.

The girl with whom he was having a fling was older than I, cute, worldly. Unfazed by this pronouncement. Apparently, that was the nature of a fling.

I wouldn't know.

Sometime earlier that month, she had shared an ice cream cone that dripped from both ends with *another* guy on our program. Walter and I had watched together, from the sidelines. It was seductive, titillating.

Neither of us commented. Walter and I just stood side by side, bemused: American college girl not given to flings and Canadian management professor at Harvard.

(This Harvard thing seems more improbable every time I revise.)

We watched the girl share a dripping ice cream cone with some guy.

On another time that Russian summer, alone with him and apparently discussing his romance—God knows where we were—I had reprimanded him, "But you have a girlfriend at home, you said?"

Walter had responded with something like, *What happens in the Soviet Union stays in the Soviet Union.*

Oh.

A Photograph of a Man and a Girl on Red Square, Moscow (July 1990)

At the Kremlin in Moscow, towards the end of the program, Walter and I stand alone again.

It's a candid shot. I don't know who took the photo or how I ended up with it.

The Twenty-Eighth Communist Party Congress is about to begin. Dan Rather is somewhere nearby. Unseen but close to us is Lenin's dead body on display.

During the past few weeks, I've eaten a hairball baked into breakfast, attended the Bolshoi Ballet, gone to the new McDonald's in Moscow. I've seen Peter the Great's palace and shadowed Raskolnikov on imagined Leningrad paths. A grayish pallor swathes the country. In the cities, tram wires crisscross overhead, and the metro reeks of infinity. Trousers with holes, ripped stockings, bad hair dye. Orwellian grocery stores with nothing on the shelves. So many serious faces—even on children. Onion-bulb tops on churches, gold-plated estates for dead Czars, palatial walls in slapdash splendor. Everyone is talking about *glasnost*, *perestroika*, and that crazy man, *Boris Yeltsin*.

It's almost over; the Iron Curtain is coming down.

Our Russian is hideous.

In the middle of Red Square, Walter—*Wall Street Journal* tucked under arm—says to me, an unglamorous girl with a hot-pink fanny pack around her waist, "Out of all the people on this trip, you're the one I'd like to know what happens to."

Grammatically awkward, unprecedented.

His comment is devoid of sexual intrigue, ulterior motive, monetary possibility.

It is the storming of my own Winter Palace.

I never see Walter again after that summer.

December 2020

There have been college degrees in unrelated fields. Irresponsible debt gave me a great education. Intellectual snobbery is a fashion accessory. I've waited for heartbreak to kill me, and, oddly, it didn't. My passport is stunning—stamped, suggestive. Drag shows in Harlem, nights on African dung floors, babies in Shanghai orphanages, hiding Cuban art in suitcases when flying out of Havana. Once, I worked at Disneyland. A man exposed himself to me in Central Park. I followed an elephant through Swazi bush. I lived in Manhattan. I crawled home to my parents. I worked at Amnesty International; there, I stole Harrison Ford's address from a Rolodex. There's been a coma. Cancered body parts removed. People once present in my life, entirely gone. The police have been summoned. Twice. I've hidden pills in drawers and cleaned up vomit. Once, I rode in an ambulance when my kid swallowed a penny. My husband can't believe I called an ambulance for that.

But I did.

There's more.

Dead dad, crazy marriage, 9/11. Not in that order.

C-sections.

Car accidents.

Cults!

Global pandemics!

Bad conversations.

When you stare, don't be too obvious.
Don't be too obvious, Walter.

Walter

But this is what I'm thinking.
Walter, where are you now?
Walter—in your knee-high yellow socks and dark blue shorts—what has become of you? Have you headed into old age with thinning hair and wrinkled skin?
Walter, the Prufrock of my Soviet Summer.
And would you recognize me today? Would you know who I am? Did you know I now fret about gray roots and living long enough to see my children marry?
Walter, I'm this other woman now.
Walter.
I like to picture us in Antwerp or Brugge. Vienna or Istanbul.
In Belgium, we'd drink beer with a trace of something raspberry; we'd eat cheese. You'd show me pictures of your kids; I'd tell you about the books I've read.
Walter.
Walter, I'd say.
Talk to me.
Tell me things.
My long lost Walter.
If you saw me now, would you recognize me?
Could you see past skin damage, my flesh in ruins?
All of our maps have changed, Walter.
Our globe, unrecognizable.
Where are you now?
Walter, when you'd throw your eyes over me as if I were naked, when you saw how time had elapsed on my face, when you tried to ignore scars that hint at disaster far worse than a hot-pink fanny pack worn on a Soviet summer so long ago—when you saw these things—after so many years, would you be disappointed?
Would I disappoint you?
My long-gone Walter.
Are you disappointed?

I Am Writing Blindly

Walter, are you disappointed?
Walter?

My Defunct Political Book: Noah Baumbach's Mom Was My Landlord

I think this is the hardest piece to write. In the fall of 2019, I took a class on Memoir Writing at Phoenix College (with Amy Silverman). Three things happened in this class. First, I planned—pretty actively—to write a full-fledged book on politics and my political experiences, discussing the weird combo of orthodoxy and secularity that dominates my thinking. Second, I discovered that I did quite a bit of writing of "collages"—bits of prose that were thematically linked but not always obviously or, um, cohesively so. However, I liked them! Third, I realized that I didn't have enough material for a whole book on the topic, or if I did, I wasn't all that interested in writing a whole book about the topic. Here, then, is the political collage that might've been a book, but isn't. This is the surviving mishmash, my rage against the machine, my crude surgery. I debated with myself whether to write it down or suck it up, let it jam my arteries or do whatever happens in those dark rivers running throughout my body. How do you write about an era without succumbing to a pedantic rant? But isn't my job to move through any landscape, political or not, story by story?

Dear Trump,

Why not write you a letter? You were, after all, the one who got me all crazy about politics again after fifteen years of brain-freeze. And there are things I want to tell you . . . .

Every ten minutes, I (moderate lefty with uber-religious convictions) feel as if I need to revise this essay, because something insane happens to send me back to the laptop.

Sigh. Exhale.

Let me be clear.

You are responsible for this piece. I would've let my political past be exactly that: *my past*. But you got me riled up, crazy. While I cruelly tell Tim that he gave me cancer (that's in another book, on sale now), I might say that you gave me high blood pressure and put me on Celexa.

But before I get too nuts . . . .

You are no Putin. I might have friends that insist on your pure villainy. I don't see it, really. Pure buffoonery, *yes*. Hitler, *no*. Dumb, *yes*. Putin, *no*.

You are not bright enough, visionary enough, skillful enough or, truthfully, evil enough.

You are just a brew of a Kardashian, a TikTok influencer, the Insurrection Dude with the Horns, O.J. Simpson, and Tom Cruise.

Let's not be overly dismissive, though: There are criminals and murderers and fools and frauds up there on that list.

Nonetheless, I write to you. Because you oughta know.

You Oughta Know.*

In the Beginning: Life on the Border, The Seventies

Abridged Version: *Hippie Jewish Parents Become Born-Again Christians.*

Well, Trump, how does it all begin? From whence did my political ambivalence and fleeting career come?

The seventies. The border. The 'rents. Hippies or Republicans? Jews or Christians? Commies or fascists? MLK or Billy Graham? Rock 'n' roll or Amy Grant?

I was in trouble from the beginning.

Why couldn't I just be a normal WASP or a nice Jewish girl, a shiksa *or* nun?

In the seventies, my parents lived in Phoenix, Arizona, in a desert tract home. The home had three bedrooms; there were many pets over the years with names like Gandhi (cat) and Baba Ram Dass (dog); my mom and dad seemed like they lived on the lam from their old life in Chicago—still pot-smoking, definitely Harry Chapin-loving, always MLK-spouting refugee/cowboys in the Wild West, far from the Windy City with its organized crime, barbecued ribs, world-class art, and domineering parents. Plus, swinging was in among their sexually revolutionized Chicago-crowd, and that wasn't their thing.

Pot, *yes*. Swinging, *no*.

---

*From Alanis Morrisette's "You Oughta Know."

Kids Without Horses

The brakes on my mom's green Volvo failed, and she drove through the carport, which is how they got a brick fireplace. Everything else about our house was ordinary, except that it was in the desert, surrounded by mountains that I didn't appreciate till I was forty-five. Dust Devils crossed our backyard, leaving a grime-coated patio. There was a swing set, a "jungle gym," from atop I once sat in my bathing suit and watched the neighbor's daughter get married in her backyard.

My dad—who looked like a Doobie Brother—didn't have a college degree, but he worked hard his whole life, and I think he wished he were rich. My mom came from money and didn't care about it till she was older. She had platinum-blonde hair and looked like a go-go dancer, like a cohort of Marlo Thomas and Mary Hartman and Cher, and Joni Mitchell, too. My mom's family owned Smoky Joe's on Maxwell Street in Downtown Chicago, which famously clothed the Jackson 5 at least once. My dad worked there. That's how they met. My parents moved away when I was three, landing in Phoenix. The city, a desert outpost, was almost quaint in the seventies. IHOP, Burger King, an amusement park called Legend City. My childhood was all Bob Dylan, Carole King, *Godspell*, *Sesame Street*, and Dr. Seuss. In Phoenix, there were drive-in movies to watch *Herbie* sequels and *The Apple Dumpling Gang*. In Phoenix, I bought stickers and fuzzy pencils at Metrocenter Mall. It was not idyllic, but it wasn't bad, either.

However, by third grade, I was a Christian kid.

Headline: *Hippie Mom Takes Philosophy Classes at a Community College, Finds Jesus.*

I mean, it all changed.

Trump, you must understand this part.

No Jews for Jesus here. We were the intellectuals, so to speak. Reformed Christianity. Calvinism. It gets tricky. My parents literally fell into the arms of the most—*what should I say?*—academic, puritanical, orthodox, straight-laced groups of Christians out there.

I sound critical and *I am* critical, but, well, I'm *still* a Reformed Christian, as I speak/write. Reformed Christians are the ones sitting in the hard-backed wooden chairs, speaking about glory.

Well, that might be another story, another book.

(Did I write that one, too? Check your libraries. Trump, I will personally suck it up and walk you through the process of getting a library card. We can talk on the phone, a burner phone, even. I can help you navigate this book thing. Let me know.)

I think it's important to inform you how this influences my politics and my feelings. Immediately—*immediately*—my convictions were oppositional. How does a hippie child balance Christianity?

How will this child vote?

I mean, Trump, I'm all pro civil rights. I'm an internationalist at heart: THIS is my heart. So I'm a liberal?

But I get the personal responsibility narrative, the notion of sin. So I'm a conservative?

But I think gun people are, like, not people I want to have dinner with. And your build-the-wall bullshit is so offensive to me that I literally cannot associate with your kind. So I'm a liberal?

But Cancel Culture gets mind-numbing, and I get critical of public education. So I'm a conservative?

Though banning books is mortifying, and I'm completely, wholly pro reading—deliberately—POC writers. Liberal?

Trump, do you see what's happening here?

Do I sit with the evangelicals in their morality, or do I stand with the oppressed and hungry?

Usually, I'm alone.

That's how it feels on the border.

It was always about Christianity.

Always about integrity.

Always about hippie parents and being born again.

Always about the Church.

Trump, how dare you pose as one of them?

How dare you?

But—this is important—if you've got hippie/Jewish parents from Chicago, you'll never fit in with the Christian crowd anyway. And you probably really won't try.

In fact, you probably won't give a crap.

Actually, that's not true.

You'll give a crap for years—until you don't . . . .

No, Trump. I just don't fit in. I'm neither Jew nor Gentile.

Trump, have you read my books? Do you think they go over well with the Libs? They smell a rat. Do you think the churchy folks are lovin' my language? My free-range tongue? Nope.

I'm seriously the one streaming church services during Covid and laughing my ass/*tuchus* off while watching *Curb Your Enthusiasm*.

I live/lived a border existence.

And that's how it all began. As any refugee will tell you, life on the border is no life at all.

Trump, what do you know about refugees?

After Jimmy, The Eighties

Trump, how do you really feel about God?

I attended a weird church school in a creepy Phoenix neighborhood with a mix of overqualified and underqualified teachers (parents) that resulted in the proliferation of the principle that one is personally responsible for one's own earthly welfare. You pull yourself up by the metaphoric bootstraps. No handouts. Work is work. Morality is morality.

Private education, parental guidance required.

Oh, man, that neighborhood was so creepy. (I'm surprised none of us went missing.)

Kids could sink or swim. Smart kids excelled. Dumb kids floundered. Actually, they disappeared—I'm not kidding—like spiders disappearing into cracks in the wall. Smart ones moved onto Stanford or East Coast colleges. Dumb kids became unwed parents. Smart kids, scholars. Dumb kids, into opiates. Smart kids, homeowners. Dumb kids, welfare recipients. I don't know what happened to the average kids.

I was a smart kid.

It's all very shitty, isn't it?

Lou-Anne Drag was a bad teacher. A nice woman, a bad teacher.

I read exactly two things in high school English: the prologue of *The Canterbury Tales* and *The Picture of Dorian Gray*.

I have no memory of reading anything else in high school English.

People were talking about Jimmy Carter. Reagan was president then, but Jimmy had been the last prez. The kids at school did what kids today continue to do in classrooms: They mimic their parents' beliefs with *passion*, albeit ill-informed passion. (Gen Z might lack the passion, though I think my eldest daughter would disagree.)

On Jimmy, in a Christian school in Arizona: *much huffing, much puffing*. He was pro-choice, and they didn't like him. (At what point, I wonder now in retrospect, do people form their own politics apart from their parents? Do they always or rarely do so?)

One kid, in an obvious parental echo chamber, pompously declared, "He's not a Christian."

For once in my life, I just *listened*. (Was this the first and last time?)

I just sat there, peering over a prologue (Chaucer), looking for drama (something besides Chaucer).

Lou-Anne looked exasperated. A bedraggled, weary woman. She always seemed a bit fed up with the tight-ass Christian community that she found herself, sadly, aligned with. I related! Even then! *(I wasn't sure why!)*

Lou-Anne liked Carter (of whom I knew nothing except that he was a peanut farmer). She whispered, "You can't say that. People *believe* things. They *experience* things. We just don't *know* . . . ." And then she faded out. Her voice was only a whisper.

We never discussed it again.

However, Lou-Anne delivered subtle messages. Jimmy Carter, Democrat, could very well be a Christian man. *And who are we to decide his fate before God Almighty?*

And, even if our position on one thing—or even two or three things—is the most cogent, does it presuppose that we are right about everything else? Are we ever wrong?

It was this moment of munificent humanity. A generosity of spirit. Truth about the human heart. There's much to unpack here!

Lou-Anne Drag taught me just about nothing—except for this.

(And I love Jimmy Carter now. *God bless Jimmy Carter.*)

Skin Color

The parking garage under the condos on Astor Street in Chicago where my grandparents lived smelled of gas fumes, and it seemed like a dark and cavernous world beneath a mysterious city. Above it—right on top of it—a luxury condo building rose high, overlooking Lake Michigan with its sail boats and bordering Lincoln Park, the site of my favorite zoo and the botanical gardens where the old man always gave me a fresh orchid to take home.

My grandparents moved from Skokie to Chicago in 1976, the Bicentennial, when I was six. They had made it big. I'd later work my way into a New York story, but I never got beyond the status of child-voyeur in Chicago.

Kids Without Horses

All the doormen and all the guys in their garage were Black. Everyone addressed these men by their first names.

I said something to my grandmother, your basic Jewish grandma, born in Chicago but undoubtedly to Tevye from *Fiddler on the Roof*—who had fled from Russia. (Both sides of my family were 100 percent Jewish—Tim and I just did that DNA thing—and they were all Russian/Ukrainian/Belarussian Jews or, like, from nearby. They seriously arrived on Ellis Island, from ransacked Russian villages—the whole shebang.) And I said it condemningly. "All of the doormen are Black."

I had noticed, I think, *I know*, an economic discrepancy between these doormen and the residents of this fancy Chicago high-rise. I also disliked—at, like six or seven—that a bunch of Black guys were, um, "waiting" on the rich, white folks. My seven-year-old self was *incensed*! I had probably just seen *Roots* on TV with my hippie parents, and I couldn't believe *this modern-day BS!*

Readers will never know my grandmother. She died a while ago, but she was not going to take my tacit, pejorative, childishness. No, she would *not*. She was sharp, incisive, witty, with starlet skin.

"It isn't as if they're not paid." Esther Bublick was also morbidly obese: her own sorrow, her own crime against humanity—a very fat and wealthy Russian-Jewish woman who mostly moved from chair to chair.

Why did I, though, see this as problematic?

"There's a Black newscaster who lives in the building, too," she told me, and that was that.

Wait. Trump, how old are you?

She was Old School, a City Girl, rich, probably kinda anti-racist for the times.

I sincerely doubt she would've voted for you.

The KKK

I think your dad had some KKK connections?

Okay, so there was that. I mean, childhood is all rock 'n' roll, *Godspell*, *Roots*, hippie stuff.

College: There I was, pretending to have fun.

Was I holding a drink?

I was standing with two frat boys at a frat party and, like the do-gooder girl I was, I had on an MLK T-shirt. I was not nearly as cocky or dismissive or blasé as I would be now. I was eager and shy. I wasn't exactly smitten with the frat boys, but I was—indeed—tripping over my own limbs to present myself as a raving beauty. No easy task.

I mean, I wanted to date a hot guy.

Trump, I know you can relate. Hot girls. Hot guys. Who doesn't want one?

That's when Drunk Frat Boy One grabbed a bit of my shirt, my beloved MLK shirt, and said, "So you like this guy?" He eyed MLK, emblazoned on my chest.

I nodded.

I said, "I do?" Like I was asking a question.

Drunk Frat Boy One, then, gave me a thumbs-up and said, "Good—because he's a good Black." He rolled his clenched fist into a thumbs-down position.

He said, "Not like that other guy."

I was pretty sure it was Malcolm X who was the thumbs-down guy, and I was trying to back away, when he got close to my face, real close, and I smelled hot beer on his breath.

We froze, eyes locked.

I was a kid. He was, too

He whispered, "You like that Black #$&k?"

Fuck, I undoubtedly thought, even then, goody two-shoes masquerade falling away.

Drunk Frat Boy Two stepped in (where had he been all this time?), and he pulled Drunk Frat Boy One away, apologizing, saying, "I'm sorry, I'm sorry."

And who could I call to get me the heck out *NOW*?

I had to get out of there.

This was not my place, my world. (Cue in the Indigo Girls: "Prince of Darkness.")

I called a friend (the famous, the infamous—in my life—*Scott Hyder*), and he picked me up in his stick-shift compact car, and I was shaken and traumatized and reeling and knowing that we are metaphysically ruined and hope is forever elusive.

The rest of the night is a blur, though I'm sure I returned to my dorm and I remember hearing rumors about KKK hoods in that frat house and burning effigies in some warped trick-or-treat costumed ritual and, basically, I went through the rest of my life thinking that house was full of racists and maybe we'd all die in apocalyptic hell fires and could we—even for one lousy second—just not be monsters to each other?

Trump, I was done with the likes of them.

By Any Means Necessary

Trump, we are New Yorkers, you and I. You may die in Florida, and I may die in Massachusetts—but we know we're New Yorkers.

Back to my story.

Innocence is lost more than once, really.

Fast forward. The Big Apple. I said I'd work myself into a New York Story. I did.

During my undergrad years, I did a semester in New York.

I was on the corner of Flatbush and Dekalb in Brooklyn: the streets frenetic with movement, cacophony—a kind of life I wanted to dip into but felt hesitant about, ill-equipped for, too white and too uncool to fully enter. Junior's Cheesecake was lighting up the Brooklyn night sky like a casino on the Vegas Strip: red, yellow, beautiful. In the mornings, I'd be watching Ozzie stand over a grill in the nearby diner sweating, smiling, flipping eggs over easy, with the medley of Jamaican/Korean/Syrian/Czech/Ugandan voices filling the air around me, while out of the corner of my eye I could see boys selling bootleg cassettes because bootleg music was still a thing and men standing on makeshift platforms shouting about end times: *The End Is Coming,* they shouted.

Brooklyn worked on me, seduced me.

I could start my New York Story elsewhere, at another spot on the map—at the Empire State Building during that same season with the skyscraper pointing up like an accusing fingertip: a cityscape, a cliché. Manhattan, wretched by day, glorious by night. From above, looking down, there is distance, a silencing of the clamor below. From above, there is a city spreading endlessly out and out and *out*: twinkling like broken glass on a beach. Beautiful, despite the ugly below.

I should begin there, yes?

Either way, it was 1991.

I begin in 1991. I was twenty-one, and I wanted to change the world—because, well, *wasn't that what we all wanted to do in 1991? Change the world?*

Spike Lee's *Malcolm X* would arrive in 1992, soon, and Brooklyn was rife with *By Any Means Necessary*. Malcolm X stuff was *everywhere*, and Spike's Joint—where one could buy Spike Lee merchandise—was within walking distance of my dorm room.

(My love of Spike Lee would last.)

Starbucks wasn't even in New York yet.

I was studying at Long Island University's Brooklyn Campus on a semester-long program called "From Urban to Global Community." Though this sounds like an overstatement, even to me, that semester probably changed the course of my life. I liked *urban*. I liked *global*.

I was hypnotized by the throb of City.

If one had asked me my politics, I would've said, "Live Aid."

I would've said, "Band Aid."

I would've said, "We Are the World."

New York *bound* me; it was my secret home, my forever home.

Now, almost thirty years later, still thinking about changing the world despite my dissolving New York euphoria, still seduced by *urban* and *global* verbiage, I consider the role of race in my life.

Malcolm X and MLK were my focus that semester in Brooklyn. It was utterly unoriginal scholarly work. I added nothing to the body of existing knowledge. Rather, my study was a Rite of Passage. *What Every White American Girl Needs to Study Before She Signs Up for an International Relations Gig*.

Which is what I was about to do.

But I'm jumping ahead.

Back to Brooklyn.

It was shockingly easy: *I made a phone call*.

"May I meet with Dr. Shabazz?" I asked. Malcolm X's widow, Betty Shabazz, worked at Medgar Evers College in Brooklyn—in the Crown Heights section. Crown Heights was the neighborhood in which a race riot between the Hassidic Jews and their Black neighbors had occurred that August.

This is what I knew about the Hassidic Jews: I had read *My Name Is Asher Lev* by Chaim Potok. I liked it very much.

I wanted to interview Shabazz. I had no set topic in mind. I wanted to hear her discuss Malcolm X and his legacy, and if he were still relevant today in the Age of Spike, and if Malcolm X was right or wrong or skewed or misunderstood or justified. I wanted her to tell me things.

Kids Without Horses

She agreed to meet.

I left early for the interview, and I took the subway to Crown Heights. I sat in a pizza parlor and had a slice, thinking how I was all *Do the Right Thing*-ish by eating my pepperoni pizza. Then, I headed over.

My Rite of Passage.

There is no record of my meeting with her.

In 1997, Shabazz died from burns over 80 percent of her body. Her twelve-year-old grandson set her Yonkers apartment on fire. The kid, named Malcolm like his grandfather, went to juvi for it. (He would later be killed in 2013 in Mexico City.)

My account of our meeting cannot be confirmed or denied.

The tapes I made are lost.

When I arrived, Dr. Shabazz was already a woman tragedy-entrenched. Her husband had been assassinated on February 21, 1965. What I expected to find that fateful Brooklyn day when I met his widow was an oracle, my idealism fleshed out. Something other than what she was.

Dr. Betty Shabazz sat behind a desk in a wreck of an office with stacks of Coke cans stockpiled around. In retrospect, I doubt I would be so awestruck by the mess I saw. I had yet to be inducted into Academia where *mess* was A-Okay. Still, she took it a step too far. All that Coca-Cola? It looked like a bunker, early Y2K-hoarding-with-mixed-up-priorities, your nagging mom's worst nightmare.

Blessed Are the Peacemakers? I came to ask.

"May I tape our conversation?" I said, shyly. I had this mini-cassette recorder, not yet obsolete. I just needed to make a little transcript.

"Yes," she said, eyeing my mini-cassette.

I pushed play. *History! I was making history!*

And what I remember most about that day is the tape recorder I lost.

"So . . .," I must've begun, trying to be articulate. I started the questioning. What have you been up to since Malcolm died? *By Any Means Necessary* still?

I put it better than that. (Barely.)

What if I told you she was crazy? She spoke nonsensically, aggressively? *My beloved* this, *my beloved* that.

I could decipher nothing else.

I was too young.

I was too green.

I was too white.

She was a storm, a whirling dervish, a precursor to the flames that would eventually kill her. And I was that skittish girl tiptoeing around Flatbush and Dekalb, mesmerized by things I didn't understand.

My beloved this, *my beloved* that.

She was wailing over the body of her dead husband, and I trembled. My hands shook. I fumbled with the recorder as if I were in the only high-stakes football game I'd ever play.

My beloved this, *my beloved* that.

After about fifteen minutes, her phone rang.

Did we freeze? Stop talking? Stare at the phone? How many moments passed, as we formed this weird Bermuda Triangle: Malcolm X's widow, me, a ringing phone?

Dr. Shabazz picked it up. "Hello?"

I turned off the recorder.

She spoke.

I sat.

She hung up, looked at me.

I pushed *record* again.

Her eyes *flashed*—no joke. "You weren't taping my conversation, were you?"

Oh, no! I stuttered.

"I turned it off!" I said.

"No, I wasn't recording," I said.

"I'm just turning it back on—" I hurried to add.

She eyed me over her desk, head lowered. "Because that was just about the Hassidics." She paused, looking suspicious. "*Peace, you know—*"

Peace, you know. . . .

She was about to explode.

Peace, you know.

I truly thought she might climb over her desk and eat me. (Cannibalism, cannibalism.) "No, I wasn't taping it."

She looked at me as if I were lying.

"It wasn't on," I repeated.

She stared hard.

I shrunk.

I practically tossed the phone in the air, trying to show her that I had just pushed *play*. Miming *I-hit-play-like-this*. Holding it before her like some sort of golden calf. *Here, see?* "I can rewind it and show you, if you'd like."

Our eyes were locked.

I was scared.

And the conversation went downhill from there.

My beloved this, my beloved that.

Peace, you know . . . .

I asked no further questions.

Trembling, I fled.

I needed to get my white butt out of Medgar Evers, out of Crown Heights, away from Black kids and Hassidic Jews, away from any hotbed of discord—because, I knew: Peace was impossible.

There could be no peace.

There would be no peace.

By Any Means Necessary was said for a reason.

You take whatever peace you can get in whatever way you have to— because cynicism prevails, and this was my induction, my Rite of Passage.

And I came out, in 1991, at twenty-one, as a cynic.

Then, I knew.

Live-Aid was a farce; Band-Aid, fantasy.

We were not the world.

That's what Betty Shabazz, in her posture and rage, her suspicion of me and my cassette recorder, told me.

Peace could not be had. There would be no peace.

I thereby launched my career in international relations.

Trump, I suspect that you can relate.

I'm Not Innocent

Well, Trump, I'm not really ready to get into it with you about race.

That same Brooklyn semester in 1991 held other memories.

A hot guy in a bar who said he was with the Israeli Secret Service (trying to pick up someone else—not me), *Paris Is Burning*, and a drag show in Harlem.

And something that embarrasses me, shames me, and mortifies me.

I'm guilty, too.

I write from the vantage point of the future.

I Am Writing Blindly

It was that same Malcolm X-MLK project in my "From Urban to Global Community" semester in 1991. Somehow or other, there was this young scholar guy, a doctoral student at Columbia who was on campus, and I asked to talk to him about my project. We met in the library of Long Island University's Brooklyn Campus.

He was a Black guy, probably in his twenties.

I can only guess, now, at my thoughts.

Was I hoping to strike up a romantic relationship?

Possibly. Ph.D. Columbia.

Was I only interviewing him because he was Black?

It could be.

Did he have anything at all to do with my project? Was he connected to MLK or Malcolm X?

I don't even know.

Was I seriously just targeting a Black guy to ask him Black guy stuff?

I kinda think so.

What *were* my motives?

We sat in the LIU library and I remember it like this: I asked, "How do you know this stuff?"

I mean, it probably wasn't *that* dumb. I find me so offensive. (How do you know this stuff?????)

Maybe I actually was hitting on him.

He paused, did not shoot me a sarcastic grin, did not reveal angst and certainly not surprise. He just said, "Well, I'm getting a Ph.D."

Or it might've gone like this:

I showed amazement at his intellectual acumen, and I said, "Wow! How do you do that?

Again, it probably wasn't *that* dumb. (But it might've been!)

He paused, collecting himself, sadly used to responses like mine. And he said, "Well, I'm getting my Ph.D."

Or it might've gone like this:

I really *was* trying to hit on him, but I was so dumb and totally unsophisticated and—as loathe as I am to acknowledge it now—tacitly racist. So I asked, "How in the world does a Black guy like you even know this big intellectual stuff?"

It probably was *that* dumb. (Lord in Heaven.)

He paused, likely no stranger to this kind of thinking, likely assessing quickly—so very quickly—in his head how to best handle this. Should he handle it loudly or subtly? Should he put her in her place, make her remember it forever, correct her, ignore her? He was maybe thinking, *She's young, after all.*

He said, "Well, I'm getting my Ph.D."

I knew what I had done.

I knew immediately.

So subtle.

This is the end of that story.

Oh, Trump. You and race. You're always just so not really in touch with the intricacies of the human condition, lacking the emotional depth and perceptive abilities to decipher what it's like to be anything other than what you seem to be: a flat character, not a round one. Am I being one-dimensional myself? Are you more than a caricature? More than an Elmer Fudd? More than a Lenny/Squiggy barging into Washington?

You just don't seem to really get it.

First, You Get the Degree

Trump, tell me about Wharton.

But me first.

The first time I voted, I voted for Dukakis.

When I found out that Bono said *fuck*, I planned on saying *fuck*, too.

At the University of Arizona, I majored in political science and creative writing. I don't know how to fully explain this. Political science was a cultural imposition, a career choice, practical (in my head). Creative writing was a compulsion, organic and impractical, a vocation.

I usually try to block this part out, but I did have one professor hint that I probably wasn't the political science type (was it that obvious?). It was during an honors American politics class in my freshman year, and I met him in his office. I can still picture him. That old dumpy academic, messy gray hair, thick black (kinda gross) mustache, skinny but with ashen skin and saggy jowls, dress shirts with yellow underarm stains, tall and slouchy. Maybe a lush (he looked like a lush, now that I think about it), maybe not. "You remind me of my daughter. Her name is Jennifer, too," he told me. *They're all named Jennifer*, I wanted to say but didn't. When I told him that I was double-majoring in creative writing, he said, "I bet you're a good writer."

I've never been able to decide if he was being creepy or patronizing—but then I remember that he's probably dead now, and I decide on patronizing.

Turned out he was right—I wasn't the political science type—though I persisted.

I moved back to New York when I left Tucson.

During my masters in politics (international relations) at NYU, I knew I wasn't the "type." New York City was perfect, but my thesis advisor also hinted that I was probably a good writer and maybe not up to this academic gig. He was this young Harvard-grad NYU faculty guy, and there was this rumor that he messed up his marriage by having an affair with a grad student. I, disaffected political scientist, registered Democrat, lousy Christian, City Slicker Exile, found this attractive in a man and spent the next couple years of grad school wondering why he wasn't interested in me.

(I just remembered that my kids are old enough to read this.)

I *think* I tried to hit on him, but neither of us could tell for sure.

(All these absurd stories about me not really hitting on guys!)

I remember a lot of game theory, which felt like another imposition to me. How could you discuss qualitative issues like good and evil in quantitative terms?

(In grad school, I learned to say things like that.)

And then I was done! (See "Closer to Fine" by the Indigo Girls again: I refer you to the whole song.)

Here begins my career in politics!

Short-Lived Career

I stayed in New York City.

To be closer to you, Trump.

Not.

I got a job.

I was not a hard worker. I did not contribute to the greater good. I was not an asset to anyone. And I'm not proud of my utter lack of professionalism.

I need to confess that, when I speak of writing as my thing, as my vocation, as the only thing I actually do well, I REALLY mean it. I work very hard at it; I am unflagging, even.

Such devotion was not part of my first career.

Kids Without Horses

I worked at Amnesty International in Campaigns.
I worked at the United Nations Association-USA.
I worked at the Council on Foreign Relations.
These were *good* places.

I stuck around for exactly two years, and it's difficult to say whether I would've become ambitious or revealed a hint of professionalism or taken any job ladders seriously had I stayed longer. My memories are not great. It was the nineties—the era of Thursday night television, of watching *E.R.*, of walking from my apartment on Greenwich Avenue all the way up to East Sixty-Eighth Street (wearing a Walkman). It was the era of *Love Slave* and Tori Amos, The Candy Butchers and the Fez Under Time Café. I stepped foot in many fascinating places; I left behind nothing, not a trace of anything. I left no dent on the City.

The writing was probably on the wall—no pun intended. It was Harry Chapin, Bono, and MLK who broke my heart. Academics immediately noted my lack of acumen. It was New York I liked best. Spike Lee was a downright romantic figure. Betty Shabazz sent me running.

I don't think there's anything else one needs to know about my early political career besides the following:

I took the Foreign Service Exam at Columbia University so I could be a diplomat, and I was right near that diner in "Seinfeld." I failed the exam by something like one point. Like, I *failed* by *one* point. Therefore, I am not a diplomat. (I think I'm acting more blasé about this than I truly felt; I wanted to work in foreign service.)

I had two business trips while working in Manhattan. On one, I went to the Twin Cities in Minnesota and, on the other, I went to Washington, D.C. Crazily, I don't remember doing work on either trip.

In Minnesota, I went to the Mall of America, ate lunch with my friend's mom (who had duck), and I remember laughing aloud while watching TV in my hotel room alone—and thinking how weird it is to laugh when no one is in the room with you: It's like that old question, "If a tree falls in the forest and no one hears it, does it make a sound?" *If I laughed aloud in a hotel room and no one was there to hear me, did I really laugh aloud?* That was my profound thought on the St. Paul/Minneapolis trip. I don't even know what I was doing in Minneapolis or St. Paul—but I know I rented a car! And I know I laughed aloud in a hotel room while alone!

In D.C, I went to many Smithsonian museums and sang karaoke with an old college acquaintance I never saw again. I do not remember what we sang. Her name was Claudia or Claudine, and I feel a little bad because I don't know.

I was pseudo-bulimic for most of my time in Manhattan, in that I binged without purging. In other words, I gained a lot of weight.

I saw many famous people. Ethan Hawke, twice. Noah Baumbach's mom was my landlord. She was very nice, and her husband plunged my toilet multiple times. Sadly, I never once saw Noah.

Yes, that's right. Noah Baumbach's stepdad plunged my toilet.

I bought new books from Barnes & Noble, read them, and returned them. I mean, it's like I spit in the face of my future life as a writer.

I wrote a bad novel that was liked by an editor at Random House, and he met with me to discuss rewrites, and I'll never forget this man (Ian) as long as I live. He was very much into my book, until he rejected it. He was British, and I love him still. I've tried to reach him now that I'm a famous writer—but it's never happened.

I "worked" in the nongovernmental organization (NGO) sector. I wanted to work in international human rights. *But I must've not wanted it that badly.* Depressing. I must've been hoping to rub elbows at cocktail parties with Sting and Aung San Suu Kyi. I pictured myself in embassies, wearing gowns. I'd be taller, thinner. But that never happened, either.

Here's a partial list of the political powerhouses I encountered during my stateside career: Andrei Kozyrev (I was into him), Madeline Albright, Hillary Clinton, Salman Rushdie (my fave to name-drop, besides Ethan Hawke), Ted Turner, Jane Fonda, Newt Gingrich, and Desmond Tutu. I can't remember the others.

(Note from the future: I recently saw Andrei Kozyrev on the news, living in Florida, an old man decrying Putin and his invasion of Ukraine. I felt an inexplicable wave of warmth for him, and joy that he was safe in Miami.)

That is the sum of my political career.

Shun Lee Palace, 1996

Ah, Donald: We have some things in common.

In Midtown, I sought illicit funds.

This was during my final year in the Big Apple.

We met, this CEO guy and I, at Shun Lee Palace on Fifty-fifth. I didn't often get to eat Chinese in New York City—only because I could never afford it. I had eaten it with a friend on a Thanksgiving because I had absolutely no plans and only Chinese was open, and I had once eaten dim sum in Chinatown with another friend though I ended up puking all night long and never eating dim sum again.

I still never want dim sum.

Do not talk to me about dim sum.

At Shun Lee, I was wearing my Gap dress and a London Fog coat, looking like a cliché of *Harried City Girl Preying on Rich Old Man*. He sat in back, surrounded by empty tables. He wasn't really smoking his stubby, stinky, soggy cigar—but my memory plays a trick. His eye twitched; was he winking or was it a medical condition?

He probably said, "Order whatever you'd like."

He probably said, "I'm not giving you money, but why South Africa?"

I had sent out letters to rich men that I found through my legit job, asking for donations so I could finance my "study" or "internship" as a writer in South Africa. *I literally asked for money to personally use on my work's letterhead.*

I. Can't. Even.

I'm not sure how I came up with this unsavory scheme.

This criminal scheme!

I had to know that I shouldn't solicit donations from associates at work. GoFundMe campaigns weren't around yet—but I knew fax machines were off limits; letterhead, too.

I had used letterhead. I had faxed the letters. This was completely illegal. Worse than using the printer in the office!

(I'm talking about this now; surely, the statute of limitations prevents prosecution. I guess I won't be running for political office, after all.)

It's hard for me to believe I did this. (I find it easier to believe that I bought new books from Barnes & Noble, read them, and returned them. That kinda sounds like me. But stooping to this level?)

I told you, Trump, we have something in common.

I ate moo shu pork at Shun Lee with a faux-mafioso guy, who probably said, "You know this is against the law?"

No one reported me; no one donated either.

This guy with the eye-twitch probably saved my life by nipping my criminality in the bud (though I did commit an international felony the following year —more later).

I had decided—with my South Africa plans—that the profs were right. I had no business in politics: *I'd be a writer! Green Hills of Africa!*

I'd leave, student-loan entrenched, subway savvy, up to my neck with sitting dramatically alone in Village cafes in which no one noticed, done with U2 who had most definitely sold out as had I, twenty pounds overweight, never having run into Noah Baumbach.

Shun Lee Guy asked me about my writing, too.

They all ask about my writing.

New York was over.

Skipping South Africa

So, like, we're going to skip this entire era, which really served as a bizarre bridge to my life as a writer. We'll jump over it, much like we jump over that bizarre allegation against you that you once stayed in the Ritz Carlton in Moscow in 2013, sleeping in the bed used by Barack and Michelle Obama, and hiring prostitutes to do some kind of "golden shower" routine. I mean, obviously something's going on there. Same with South Africa. We'll let it go.

I really did become a writer!

Prager Years, 2004–14

Funny to think about this now.

I guess I went Republican before you.

I married a Republican in my thirties.

I know, right?

Let's call the next decade *The Prager Years*. Buried up to my neck in disposable diapers, I reverted to otherworldly lethargy. Politics sucked, the world sucked, people sucked: *Forget this place.*

The Prager Years were cynical years.

I gave up.

Gen X has nothing on the tongue-clucking of a good conservative.

This is, I say it now, the fatal flaw of conservatism gone wrong (it can go right): not giving a damn. Saying: *Screw this place.*

Or: *We can't do anything.*

Yes, it was the Age of Terror, post 9/11.

Basically, when I gave up on the world, I went Republican. My cynicism led to conservatism.

This is really how I feel now.

Somehow, the change in airport security, the pessimism of my own loneliness in a then-unhappy marriage, the lack of outside stimulation, the cockiness of Reformed Theology (yeah, I said that, too), and my fears surrounding being the worst mother in the world resulted in a kind of giving-up-of-the-ghost. I did what I thought I had to, everything I thought I'd never do: *I succumbed to rigid orthodoxy.* Riding the evangelical bandwagon, turning off my NPR, I listened to Dennis Prager without mercy. I had no time for the sorrows of others.

My new crime: lovelessness, moral stupor, self-interest.

I said, "I'm apolitical."

I suppose that sounded better than: "I give up."

I feel a bit bad about blaming Prager. I think he's a nice guy.

How had Christianity landed me here?

Didn't I know better?

Philando Castile, 2016

Cancer saved me. Or maybe you did.

On July 6, 2016, Philando Castile was pulled over by cops in Minnesota and shot seven times in front of his girlfriend and her daughter.

I was in remission. He was dead.

What, then, is real criminality?

Is it criminal to look at the world around you—a world in which Black men are killed in cars by cops in front of four-year-old girls, a world in which four-year-old girls say to moms in the back of police cars, "I don't want you to get shooted"—is it criminal to look away?

Do conservatives look away?

Had I looked away?

But it got worse: You were running for president.

Could character be criminal?

Could my vote be criminal?

I'm Back!

I don't know what would've happened had it not been for you.

I really don't know.

You seduced my people.

You made a fool of my people.

It's one thing for me to cuss and be published by Christians.

It's quite another for you to weaponize Jesus Christ.

I had to get up; I had to gather my Jewish girl *Chutzpah*, my Reformed Christian elitism, my U2-Infused internationalism, my MLK-T-shirt-wearing ways, and I had to say, "No fucking way."

I Went to One Rally, Back in 2016

I cannot remember the first moment that I became aware of your bid for the presidency. I'm sure I was dismissive, like everyone else I knew. Then, when it seemed *real*, like you were really going to do this, I believed—like everyone else I knew—you'd lose.

I do remember driving home, literally turning onto Cactus and heading east towards Seventh Street, thinking to myself, *Voting for Hillary is the only moral choice.*

That's what I thought.

We attended one rally. I went to the Phoenix Civic Center in downtown Phoenix in October 2016, pulling my girls out of their private Christian school—which had, until that year, seemed mostly removed from partisan politics. I was taking my kids to see Michelle Obama—because she was a mom, too, she was beautiful, she was fun, and she was smart. The girls were excited because they got to leave school and Michelle had danced on Jimmy Fallon. We ran into an old friend with whom I went to college, who was with *her* two kids—plus the whole vibe was celebratory. We were on the winning side! A stage, crowds, placards, balloons, TV cameras.

We were the good guys!

The next day, my girls returned to school. I sent photos to their teachers.

One responded with a "That's so great!" comment. (I'd subtly figure out that she was on *our* side.) She had to be careful. She might've realized before I did that the Christian church would be divided.

The other teacher never responded, but soon, a photo of another little girl at a Trump rally showed up on the teacher's bulletin board. Smiling away.

That little girl got to be on the bulletin board.

I was hurt.

On my children's behalf?

(They didn't care.)

I said nothing. I mean, what was I going to say?

It didn't taint our experience at the rally.

My girls truly didn't care that they weren't put on the bulletin board, too.

I cared.

How to explain this here, story by story?

How to explain the pang, the alienation, the sense of aloneness I would feel?

How to explain that my people, my true people, the people with whom I stepped into a parted Red Sea, the family with whom I wandered the desert and with whom I took bread and the cup had betrayed me, betrayed my God, by justifying this vote as the right thing to do in a bad situation?

How could I explain that it felt like brokenheartedness?

That I had a broken heart?

Like throwing down the Ten Commandments on the ground at Mount Sinai and watching the tablets break into pieces?

That I was never the same again?

I was never the same again.

Evangelical Became Partisan

Now, we're simply talking about you.

I told Tim, "You will break my heart if you vote for Donald Trump."

You will break my heart, I said.

What compelled me to go there? What made this so critical, so crucial? Why would I bind his very conscience? I never had done that before—to *anyone*. What made this situation unique? Why did I dare go that far?

So, well, he didn't vote for Donald Trump.

(*You can only use this line the first time around*, I joked with a friend who was married to a conservative, too.)

In September of 2016, the guy from Latinos for Trump famously said, "If you don't do something about it, you're going to have taco trucks on every corner."

Tim didn't work on Election Day, so we ate lunch at a taco truck. We were jubilant, excited, celebratory. We started watching the news as soon as the polls closed.

In 2016, Tim spared my heart.

But I went to bed early, sad, stunned.

You won.

Hell is for Theorists

If I talk theory, I'll lose everyone.

I think I need to explain why I'm a moderate.

Look, I know my audience: mostly liberal, often academic, typically urban. Some stragglers, a few conservatives, loyal friends, my mom. Do I risk losing people with the smarmy, highfalutin talk?

Here:

This is theory.

Liberals philosophically embrace the idea that human nature is essentially good.

Conservatives embrace the idea that human nature is flawed (fallen).

This is something that liberals need to know about conservatives, and conservatives need to know about liberals: *We all want world peace.*

I'm almost done with the theory part.

Liberals want world peace, and it is their understanding that all of us need to address the bad stuff. Government can help fix things. We can get schools in order. We can support government programs that address homelessness or children in poverty or global health pandemics. We can impose good measures. *Government is a tool in taking care of people.*

Conservatives want world peace, too, and it is their understanding that we cannot impose externalities to fix internal sin problems. Hearts need to change for us to see real change. Individuals need to get with it and feed the poor, take care of their neighbors, teach their children well. It's not about government taking care of people; less is more. *People take care of people.*

I'm a liberal; I'm a conservative.

Life on the border. I live on the border.

Theory section: *Over and out.*

My Criminal Record

Since you're a felon and all, I thought I'd confess to my crimes (besides illegally soliciting funds) right here.

Kids Without Horses

I drank alcohol underage. I have minimal memory of big incidents because I never cared all that much about drinking, ALWAYS preferring cheesecake and mochas.

I made countless copies on office copiers (it's horrible); I sent personal emails while on the job; I made long-distance phone calls at work—back when that was a thing.

I stole a lot of time.

I have no memory of stealing office supplies, but I'm sure I ate more than my share of free food at the office.

I was once in the parked car when the guy I was dating bought pot from his dealer in Cape Town, South Africa. So I guess this is an international crime. *I did sit there, having one of those moments in which you see yourself from above: You look down, you are in a car, the window is rolled up, you are looking out, you are hating your life and who you are. This probably belongs in the cannibalism piece in South Africa.*

I smoked the pot—not a lot. This appealed to me even less than drinking.

This reminds me, however, that I once drove a getaway car when my friend stole Mickey Rourke's leather jacket off a film set in the early nineties in Tucson, Arizona.

I also stole a rock from my neighbor's rock collection in her backyard when I was four or five. I snuck into her yard, and it was a total failure because my mom saw me through the kitchen window. My mom made me return the rock within ten minutes, so this barely counts. (It must've been some rock!)

Isn't it funny how kids collect rocks? Trump, did you collect rocks?

I snuck into the film, *The Doors*, with a friend. After our own movie finished, rather than exiting through the lobby, we crashed the Val Kilmer film. That was in 1991 (busy year!). It was a Harkins theater in Phoenix, near a now-defunct Tower Records where I saw the late Dolores O'Riordan, lead singer of the Cranberries, sing a cappella like an angel.

I was with friends in Europe in a café in Zagreb, still Yugoslavia back then, when one of us altered a Eurorail pass to extend it a few days or weeks. Another international crime!

And now that I think about it, I've shamelessly and regularly trespassed on private property, like the guy on the surveillance video who some say is Ahmaud Arbery when he walked around that construction site in Georgia, shortly before he was killed by a father and son combo.

I have no real criminal record.

But I have gotten away with many crimes.

Cancel Culture, in a Nutshell

I'm not giving up Sherman Alexie, Junot Díaz, Ernest Hemingway, Flannery O'Connor, or Harriet Beecher Stowe. And there ain't no way on Earth I'm getting rid of my Dr. Seuss books.

I only read the first Harry Potter book by J.K. Rowling, but my kids read them all. Look, the Christians wanted to ban her, and I didn't. The Left wants to cancel her and I won't.

I hated that follow-up Harper Lee book, but I'll deal. Why'd she have to mess with my Atticus?

I stopped watching Woody Allen films because they were sounding like repetitive, sexually obsessed nihilist excuses for pervs.

I forgive Aziz Ansari, because I'm inclined to do so.

Louis C.K. will likely continue to gross me out, though I did see some funny stuff from him.

Kevin Spacey seems nuts, and I'm not interested.

Bill Cosby = no intellectual/spiritual/emotional space in my head or heart for him.

Did you ever see the video of Morgan Freeman ogling the reporter? I forgive him. Old man stuff.

Remember the sex scandal with Rob Lowe five million years ago? So tame now.

I love Chick-fil-A, Netflix, Starbucks, and Target.

Hobby Lobby just has the poster boards I need at times. The store seems expensive and the books on display in the front always seem trite, but I need markers for school projects.

The Office is my favorite show of all time. I stand by it. I think often about the microaggression discourse, though.

I once got in trouble for teaching a James Baldwin book.

I once got in trouble for teaching *The Book Thief.*

I'll really go to battle over Mark Twain.

I actually did prevent my kids from reading Judy Blume (*don't shoot me*).

I wish my girls wanted to watch *All in the Family*, but they're not interested.

Same with *The Jeffersons*.
I kinda have a problem with Tom Cruise, so there's that.
I don't have a problem with Elisabeth Moss, and what does that mean?
When I think about Michael Jackson, I only get sad.
I'm okay with renaming streets and schools and removing statues. That's fine. We don't need them. Just do it peacefully.
I still love *Hamilton*.

By 2024, You Are Still Here

So I left politics once, twice, three times?
    I persist in my #NeverTrump ways.
    I decided to become a writer!
    And this is my defunct book.
    Goodnight, stars.
    Goodnight, air.
    Goodnight noises everywhere.*

---

*from Margaret Wise Brown's *Goodnight Moon*

Dear Rick Springfield

This, written in November 2012, is an unsent fan letter that appeared on my dead blog. I wrote it in response to reading the 2011 memoir, Late, Late at Night. *As far as I know, Rick never read my blog.*

Dear Rick,

    Seriously, Rick. You wrote this by yourself?

    Don't be insulted. I just didn't see it coming. I think you're fragile, actually, and I don't want to hurt you. I was impressed with your writing. I gotta be honest: It wasn't stellar, but I was definitely interested. *Absorbed*, even.

    But that's because we've got history. So, yes, I read your memoir, *Late, Late at Night*. I figured I owed it to you. Of course you owe it to *me* to read my books, as well, but (1) that's another story, and (2) I won't hold you to it.

    I decided to write this "review" in the form of a fan letter. Ironically—given my obsessive personality—I've never written a fan letter before. It's fitting that it's for you.

    I loved you so much! You were my first and second concerts (not counting Captain & Tennille)! I watched *General Hospital* for you (mostly)! I coerced my classical music-loving piano teacher to listen and analyze with me your 1985 album, *Tao*. Little did I know, you were probably spiritually done with Taoism by the time the album came out. And there I was trying to decipher your religious meanderings, your spiritual inclinations—and the Taoism phase was already kaput! You had moved on to meditation or positive thinking or a chickenless diet!

    Shortly after forcing you on my piano teacher, I was told to quit piano (by little voices in my own head), and, well, I stopped listening to your music completely. The two are probably not related. It just turned out that I had no musical talent whatsoever—and you and I, um, were just not meant to be. After a brief but meaningful fling with Duran Duran, I met U2. We've been together ever since.

You should've seen what happened when I asked my husband to pick up your book at the library for me. I had two books on hold, yours and a "legit" book of literary fiction. I didn't tell him what he was retrieving for me. I got home, and the two books—yours and the legit one—were stacked on the counter, yours on the bottom. On the top literary one, the yellow Post-it note said, "Whatever." I lifted it off the pile. On your memoir, the yellow Post-it said, "You're fucking kidding me."

But, thank you, Rick, because he was so jealous that he was pretty much Mr. Attentive for one whole night.

The analogy of a romance works. We had a romantic relationship, Rick. I grew out of it. I read your memoir, though, because of my long-standing affection for you and our complicated history.

I had thoughts.

First, I *was* impressed. My initial response was to figure out who your ghostwriter was. Apparently, there isn't one. I'm still a little surprised about this. Like it or not, you're the teen idol from the eighties—not some writer! Besides your use of big words, your storytelling instincts were good: dialogue, showing rather than telling, *blah blah blah*. So, if no ghostwriter, who's your editor?

Second, your memoir is dubbed as "searingly candid" in just about every place. And my novel is dubbed "wincingly candid" in many places, too (*was I the one who dubbed it that?*). I like to remind people about this label whenever possible.

We must hold onto this.

Third, I'd be willing to bet that, though my own preteen hormones drew me in your direction (by the way, you still look *great*!), your constant spiritual wrestling really kept me interested. I like a man who wrestles. That said—here comes the backhanded compliment thing—you could probably wrestle a little harder.

Oh, cruelty!

Fourth, you're *old*, man! When I loved you, I was eleven, twelve, thirteen. You were a grownup, doing all kinds of grownup things!

Fifth, your wife is a saint. I don't really know why the hell she stays with you—some of us make it, and some of us don't. Though you've been a lying/cheating/bastard, I am proud of your longstanding marital "success." I wish you the best.

I Am Writing Blindly

Sixth, there were things I just didn't love all that much. Your dog-love didn't work for me. And you should know that I'm a total, full-fledged, animal-loving *freak*! Dare I say, you went a little overboard?

I've said nothing about your music. You identify yourself fully as a musician. I respect that. Rock on. Keep Barbara. Find peace.
Love,
Jennifer

Not My First Time (2018)

The Quivering Pen *was a regular e-newsletter/literary blog by author David Abrams, writer of multiple books. Appearing on November 26, 2018, this was my THIRD appearance on his feature about first-time publishing experiences, called "My First Time." I wrote about my third book, which was published under dire circumstances. The original publisher dissolved her business two seconds prior to my publication—and I was forced to self-publish, which hurt in three ways simultaneously: my street cred was lost, my pride was hurt, and book sales weren't great. In all honesty, I'll never self-publish again. But I think I'll always love* And So We Die, Having First Slept *best.*

This is not my first time.

What did I think back then, with that first book, seeing my name in print? Was I all blushing bride, bookish rube? Did I carry around ink and quill just in case a random fan asked for an autograph? Was I wearing a black beret, tilted strategically on the top of my head? Did I sleep in that beret?

Tell me I didn't wear sunglasses inside.

What had I expected that first time? Accolades? A writer's retreat in, say, Bora Bora?

I guess, in all honesty, I thought it would be easier. Someone—some successful writer guy—told me in so many words, "You only come out of the gate once."

These words *hurt*. I wish I could say they didn't. *But I am haunted.*

I love my first two books. I feel strongly about them; each marks and commemorates an epoch in my life. There's something unrepeatable about their contents. When I was a kid—like a young child—I declared to my mostly stable parents, "I want to live an episodic life." Who knows what I meant? I had some kind of latent aversion to what I deemed "a white-picket-fence life." Apparently, I craved emotional upheaval and heartbreak and mental terrorism. Thinking about my childish desires now, I cringe.

Ironically, I got a rather episodic existence after all. Long story.

The Freak Chronicles is one aspect of my youth (I'm an expatriate!); *Love Slave* is another (I'm a New Yorker!). I seldom revisit either work, but when I do, I'm struck by a few things: I am not the woman who wrote either of those books, and I could not write them today (both were written several years before their publication in 2012). I last dipped into *Love Slave*, and it was really like a museum piece to me. I read it and felt almost grateful for its detail and—I'm gonna say it about my own work—*authenticity*. Here was a souvenir of my early adulthood, and I could give it to my children someday. I nailed it! And that's what I like to do: live through something (usually traumatic) and write about it later. Fictionalizing a truth and worrying over its detail.

But I'm on the cusp of publishing my third book. It's been six years since my big break. I'm this other woman now. I'm forty-eight, almost forty-nine. I've been married for fourteen years (looooonnnnnnggggg episode—we keep renewing our contract, sorta like *The Walking Dead*).

There are children involved.

I think, often, about *leaving them my possessions.*

When I die, what will my kids get?

I'll leave souvenirs, books.

You only come out of the gate once . . .

Unless you do it in a different way.

I'm coming out again?

True, the *eccentric writer routine* has lost much of its charm. (I still play it up at home. I *am* pretty weird.) I can no longer get away with certain behaviors. Any fashion statement is inevitably a bad fashion statement. It's bitterly hard to be blasé or aloof or whatever it is I'm supposed to be these days as a sexy but earthy/strong but delicate/#MeToo-conscious middle-aged woman with humility, wit, and a new book—especially when I'm just wondering what my kids are doing and if Tim managed to record *Better Call Saul* before we turn on *The Great British Baking Show*.

I *am* an eccentric writer.

But I'm *not* a cool eccentric writer.

And so, this gate that I'm supposed to walk through AGAIN . . . it's there. I see it. I'm approaching it. I'm weathered. I'm another woman.

Kids Without Horses

Make way: *Mom is a-coming.*

There's the book promo hustle. To say that I'm jaded would be too strong, too fierce. I'll only say that I worked with very talented people on my earlier books, and I had high hopes. I don't think I was planning on economic prosperity (Tim was). Rather, I think I hoped that those gates would be left wide open for me. Maybe I thought there would be people on the other side always beckoning me, calling out, "We want you! We want you!"

(In Tim's head, it was like this: *We'll pay you! We'll pay you!*)

A note on my husband who doesn't write: Tim is super supportive of my "career." I really cannot complain. I joke—*a lot*—about how he's my Sugar Daddy. There is absolutely no way I could write like I do under other circumstances. He has essentially given me a writer's life. All of that said, you know what I was hoping for when I came out of that first gate? Some legitimacy. I wanted everyone to know—even him—that *I'm working hard here. Even though it looks like I'm sitting around on the couch with the dog, I'm writing books!* I wanted to justify having a Sugar Daddy. That's not cool to say, is it?

But now what do I want for my new book?

I don't need the legitimacy. I'm past that. *I yam what I yam*, as Popeye once wisely said.

Rather, I want to commemorate another epoch. I want to fictionalize a piece of myself. I want to give it to my children.

I want to nail it.

I am overly conscious of my own mortality: That's where I am now. It's all about my children.

And Tim.

I want to say to him: *Here, I wrote you this book.*

You can show it to the kids later.

Yes, I'm rather morbid.

So is that all I want for my book? Am I looking for paparazzi and panel discussion invites, as well?

No, but here is one other thing I want:

I want to say a few things, and I'd like to say them well.

That's what I want for this book.

I may end up repeating this line elsewhere: *This is the book I wanted to write.*

Should I add "right now"?

I Am Writing Blindly

    I'm in the process of writing a piece on Elena Ferrante, but I'll say now that I guess I wish I could be somewhere between Marilynne Robinson and Elena Ferrante on the publishing front. I'd like to be wise and good like Robinson and removed from my books like Ferrante. With my other two books, I was giddy—tripping over my own two feet—to be liked for my writer self. Now, maybe a bit tempered, I admire the quiet morality of Robinson and the philosophical anonymity of Ferrante.

    Alas, I'll tell you the truth: I probably still want to be liked.

    But I'd prefer if you just liked my book.

    This is not my first time.

Casa Padre

Written for a February 2020 Roosevelt Community Church blog—prior to the Covid pandemic and the death of George Floyd—I thought I might write a series of church blog posts called "The Election Diaries," for the months leading up to the election. This piece focused on a Walmart-turned-detention-center-for-unaccompanied-minors in Brownsille, Texas. In future pieces, I thought I'd tackle topical issues. This blog idea, though, got side swept by history.

A former Walmart.

Now, a detention center in Brownsville, Texas for unaccompanied minors, "illegals."

It's hard to picture this dystopia. How do kids become unaccompanied? How are they separated from brown-skinned parents, aunts, "coyotes" paid to get kids across dusty borders? Does the child get lost in a crowd on the Mexican border? Are people running through the desert, being chased by Americans with guns? Do they fall in the dust, and do their moms scream, but someone pulls them away in the chaos? Is it winter because winters are mild on the border? Or is it summer because skies are clear and nights are temperate despite days that kill everything under the blazing, unforgiving, uncompromising sun? Where are we when it happens? Do U.S. officials wear sunglasses, like motorcycle cops? What kind of hats do they wear? Can we see their badges? Their eyes? Is it a night with roving searchlights or are people blinded, as if onstage for their big number?

I can't fully picture it.

Sometimes, I try.

* * *

I've almost lost a child twice.

I Am Writing Blindly

First, on my eldest daughter's third birthday, we put together a small party at that huge park in Anthem, Arizona. Anthem is like a pre-fabricated home; it's a pre-fab suburb or "community." It doesn't seem to have organically "risen up" out of Phoenix. I don't actually know what I'm talking about, but I get a *Stepford Wives* vibe. I'm a little weirded out by it, in all honesty.

That crazy, big park: What a great place for a kid's birthday party, though!

I've always sucked at typical mom stuff, like throwing parties or making baked goods or cutting construction paper. So this was a big deal, this event. I'd try to be normal *for her*.

We had food, drinks, cake, blankets, friends, lawn chairs.

But my three-year-old child disappeared into the maze of slides, bridges, and ladders of the Anthem park. I can see the tailspin, the panic, the taking off maniacally, the picturing of predators swooping in.

My husband took off, too, searching.

I moved into the maze, frantic.

We dropped the pretense of a party and scattered.

I remember this: *We dropped the pretense of a party.*

I couldn't do it. I couldn't be this kind of normal mom in a *Stepford Wife* prefab suburb. My baby was gone!

Ten minutes: *It was only ten minutes.*

We found her; she was fine.

That was the first time I lost a child.

Had I been negligent?

Was I a bad mother?

The second time was in a grocery store parking lot when my youngest, the other child, was six. We were done shopping, we left the store, I put everything into the trunk, and we got into the car to leave.

I locked the doors and started the ignition!

One big problem: My daughter wasn't inside the car with us.

My six-year-old was outside of the locked car!

I didn't put the automobile in reverse, okay?

There was a frenzied pounding on my window. I turned, and there was my own child, my own six-year-old daughter, screaming, "Mommy! Mommy!"

Yes, I locked my baby out of the car and almost drove off.

(*Not really: I would've figured it out.*)

Now, we laugh about it.

Kids Without Horses

I say, *Remember that time I almost abandoned you at the grocery store?*
She says, *Remember that time you tried to get rid of me?*
She knows I wouldn't abandon her.
She knows I'd only leave her against my will.
I need to ask again: What kind of mother am I?

* * *

I teach college kids in Arizona.
A few of my students are DACA students. *Dreamers*, if you will. "Illegals," if you want.
Recently, one student—not DACA—wrote that he'd seen a few detention centers. *They're not that bad*, he said.
I wondered how he managed to see these centers, though I didn't ask. But, mostly, I thought about his words: *They're not that bad.*
Like a refrain, a song.
They're not that bad.
They're not that bad.
What did he see or not see that would make him think that?
They're not that bad.

* * *

Walmart is permanently etched into my brain in the same place where I store "Unpleasant Memories From Early Marriage." I have so many Walmart stories, and they make it into every publication, much like Ethan Hawke does.
The first time I went into a Walmart was on my honeymoon. And it seems, now, as if every vacation involves at least one trip to one.
I hate the smell, the rush of hot air upon entering with the dirty cart, the underpaid and elderly greeters who can't retire, the meth lab atmosphere with the bruised produce and Equate brand of everything.
I suppose it's a great spot to detain unaccompanied minors.
Kids with lousy moms like me.

* * *

My cousin works for ICE.

I Am Writing Blindly

My cousin!

He's older than I and we were never that close, though I remember the admiring gaze I cast over him because he was so cool and it was the late-seventies and he was a nice guy.

Plus, one fine day, he introduced me to Bruce Springsteen.

The Boss.

Yes, it was him.

I am forever grateful, and this is true.

I love Bruce Springsteen, and I owe this to my cousin who now works for ICE.

Crazily, he ended up moving to the South (we're from Chicago!) and working in immigration.

The South?

ICE?

Um, really? We're like Big City Yankees! Bruce is from Jersey!

We lost touch for decades, finding each other on Facebook during the 2016 presidential elections.

Not a good time to get reacquainted.

For either of us, I would guess.

Eventually, I blocked him.

* * *

When my child was only a toddler (the grocery store one), we headed to Walmart (probably). Another trip for groceries. My kids were little, and I was a full-time stay-at-home mom.

All I did those first years of motherhood was put them in cars, go to Walmart, and return home.

Buffalo Springfield's "For What It's Worth" was playing on the car radio.

It's time we stop/Hey, what's that sound?/Everybody look, what's going down?

I had both kids in the car. One looked out the window. The toddler did her trademark three-finger trick. She, too, looked out the window meditatively, sucking two fingers and sticking a third into her nose.

It was very complicated trick she knew how to do.

Buffalo Springfield played.

Kids Without Horses

She literally pulled her fingers out of her mouth and nose, and called out to me up front in the driver's seat, "Could you turn this up?"

And then her fingers returned to her mouth and nose.

I eyed her through the rearview mirror, amused.

Could I turn it up?

I was charmed.

She really liked this song?

What a crack-up!

She was, like, two!

I turned up the volume to Buffalo Springfield.

* * *

I hadn't noticed my child slip away at a suburban park.

I hadn't noticed that I locked the doors on my child in a crowded parking lot.

I didn't even notice.

Soon, there'd be cages for kids.

Would I have been paying attention?

Would I have seen anyone moving in cots or erecting cages or blocking empty aisles in a Walmart? Would I have cocked my head in wonder or asked any questions?

Would I have been paying attention, with all my talk about a border-existence?

All my talk....

My brash talk.

Soon, there'd be rogue Springsteen fans carrying guns, imposing law and order, watching the border.

Does my cousin still listen to Springsteen?

Baby, we were born to run?*

Did he move on, "mature" now, and switch to praise-and-worship?

What would he think of me playing Buffalo Springfield with my babies in the backseat?

Later, I'd play them Led Zep, Prince.

I never said I was a good mother.

My toddler asked, "Could you turn this up?"

Would I stop, look around?

*From Bruce Springsteen's "Born to Run."

Ask about the sound?

If I had seen those detention centers for myself, would I have said, like that one student of mine, *They're not that bad?*

They're not that bad.

Would I?

Would I?

Would I?

Meningioma

I truly do think I will be in California when the Big One hits. I expect a tornado to sweep over Oklahoma when I'm in town. If we go to Cape Cod in Massachusetts, there will be a Great White attack. Maybe I shouldn't include this piece. Nonetheless, I do. But you really don't want to be in the same city as I am EVER. (I wrote this piece as I finished up my fourth book on my—you guessed it—cancer experience.)

The odds of multiple life-altering disasters befalling the same person are minimal, right?

I could never tell if my cancer memoir was really done.

After all the surgeries, the chemo, the radiation, and the reconstruction, the oncologist gave me "the talk" about forsaking the pattern of being propelled from disaster to disaster. Life would no longer be punctuated by doctor appointments. Presumably, normal life would return. I ended my memoir. Treatment over, book done.

Right?

But I spent a lot of time thinking about the end of my memoir.

How does a memoir end? Should the author die?

And my philosophizing on ends gave over to thoughts on Art.

I wondered: *Do I believe* damage *is necessary for Art?*

My cancer book isn't about disease, is it? It's about ruins, body parts, identity. I'm doing a kind of papier-mâché, a form of pointillism. I've rolled up sleeves, exposed track marks. I've charged laptop batteries, poured coffee, pet the dog, moved the cat, sat down, written the ugly.

Damage, my medium. Disaster, a theme.

Didn't James Franco make *The Disaster Artist*?

It's the title, really.

Must disaster give way to calm if an end is to be had?

I Am Writing Blindly

* * *

A meningioma is a benign brain tumor. It grows slowly, oft undetected. Sometimes, it presses on the brain. There might be seizures. Dementia. Other things.

* * *

As a teenager, I declared, "I don't want a white-picket-fence life." Was it an allergic reaction to the American Dream? Premature angst? "I want an episodic life," I added.

As for the literary implications, maybe I had an early, latent interest in plotting or narrative or Freytag's Pyramid.

Probably, I'd seen too many Duran Duran videos. First, I'd be in Sri Lanka; then, Antigua. I'd wear fedoras, my head tossed back in laughter, like a Nagel painting. White teeth. As Simon Le Bon sings, *Her name is Rio and she dances on the sand!**

Just let my life be an adventure, I was saying.

* * *

In Janet Burroway's *Writing Fiction*, she says, "[O]nly trouble is interesting."

What I didn't know in my Jordache jeans adolescence is that my wish for episodes was a wish for trouble.

Sample life episodes might be the following:

Childhood: "I Was Too Young When I Saw *The Unbearable Lightness of Being*."

New York: "I'm A Single Woman Living in a Gay Neighborhood and I Love Your Dog."

World Travel: "I Am a Citizen of the World, So I Am Alienated and Belong Nowhere but Want Good Food."

Marriage: "Babe, I'm Gonna Leave You—I Ain't Joking."**

* * *

---

*from "Rio."
**from Led Zeppelin's "Babe I'm Gonna Leave You."

Kids Without Horses

Cancer, I'll Give You One Year was finished when I took my eldest daughter to see *Hamilton* for her birthday in February 2018. Just the two of us. There was a new, "heavy" feeling in the back of my head. I'd been talking about frequent headaches.

The balcony was daunting. Surprisingly, I didn't accidentally plunge over the edge onto the season ticket holders below.

Cheap seats.

But my head hurt.

Hamilton was great.

That weekend, Tim and I also watched *Get Out*. I couldn't believe all the hype over that dumb movie.

I called the doctor on Monday.

My oncologist ordered an MRI.

Once you get cancer, everything is cancer.

* * *

Within hours of the MRI, my oncologist called. "Don't panic," he said.

I saw a neurologist the next day.

We went home from the neurologist's office, packed a bag, and drove straight to the hospital—where brain surgery was immediately scheduled: a probable meningioma.

Get Out, indeed.

I'd miss the big used book sale at the Arizona State fairgrounds that year.

My kid had a school trip to Kartchner Caverns in a week. I was supposed to be a chaperone.

Was this normal life? An episodic existence?

Did that mean my book was unfinished after all?

Would I die at the end?

* * *

My one-time neighbor, Selma, had brain cancer when I was younger. She was a brilliant lawyer beforehand, I had heard. I never knew her prior to the cancer, though. After surgery, she was sweet, unable to work or read or even follow a TV show. She was slow moving, still alive, wanting to be alive. Her desire to live was always what I found striking. Her husband's job transferred to another state, and—just like that—they were gone. She left with him, having no other choice.

I wonder sometimes, *Is she still alive?*

I always said that, if it were me, I wouldn't operate. Not the brain. I'd die instead.

But here I was, preparing for brain surgery.

After a brain injury in 1998.

(Maybe I, too, was once a brilliant lawyer—but they just don't want to remind me.)

Brain surgery.

Would *Get Out* be the last movie I ever saw? *Really?*

How could I miss work since I'm an unknown writer living off my husband? I couldn't miss work!

I was reading *Olive Kitteridge*; didn't that figure?

I wrote Tim and the kids messages to read, in case I died.

He wouldn't read them; he never read them.

I told his sister on the phone, "If I don't make it, I need you to fly out here."

* * *

When I decided to write about cancer, I decided *not* to write about medical procedures. So here are four facts about my brain surgery, rather than all of the very gory, alien-esque/wormy details:

A. They couldn't find a good vein for my IV. They tried each arm, both wrists. Finally, the jugular. *Stick it in*, I shouted. The IV went into my jugular. Seems fitting.

B. My neurosurgeon was assisted in surgery by his wife. Two brain surgeons! I tried asking personal questions about this since it's utterly fascinating to me, but I got nothing. Weird marriage. I hope it was a good day for them, no simmering tension or underlying sorrows. I simply can't fathom Tim and me doing that. I doubt we could successfully collaborate on carving a turkey.

C. After surgery, I lost taste for weeks! No one told me that this would happen, so I was taken by surprise. I was very sad about coffee. I never stopped drinking it, though—ever persistent in my bad habits. My taste buds came back on a Taco Tuesday!

D. It was not cancerous. I spent one freakin' day in ICU with an IV in my jugular. I tried to watch *La La Land* to make sure I survived past *Get Out*. That sucked, too. I might be the only person in the world who disliked both of those films.

And then I went home.

I actually taught in-person college classes that Monday. Brain surgery on Friday, class on Monday. (Tim and I needed to afford Netflix and Amazon Prime, after all.) I still went to Kartchner Caverns with my kid as a chaperone, as well.

Just another episode.

* * *

I did not include my meningioma in the cancer book. In truth, I find it embarrassing. Like, *really*?

I can, it seems, always top *crazy* with *crazier*.

Originally, I wrote about three or four epilogues. Finally, I settled on one.

But cancer taught me about Art and the episodic life.

And about Disaster.

And now, moving past *Get Out*, I'm still thinking about endings.

Are there discrete and separate ends to each of life's episodes, or do they bleed into each other?

Is my job as *artiste* to "impose" an end?

Is the necessity of an end a philosophical statement?

I think, now, how disaster has carved out episodes, episodes have shaped me, and damage has been done. I also think of the way damage has birthed art, and words have sprung forth from tumors.

Do I believe Damage *is necessary for Art?*

As much as I want to deny it, I can only say, *I do* and *I do* and *I do*.

Do I believe in the end?

I do and *I do* and *I do*.

Just not today.

V

An Ode to David Sedaris

I might confess to favoring a kind of literary aesthetic. I dub it "The Candor Aesthetic." I guess I'd say that I like an up-close-and-personal kind of prose. Others might use the words raw *(overused, can be embarrassing, I take it still) or* honest *(I've gotten* in-your-face *too. Unsightly?). It's easier to point to it than it is to define it, maybe. I was blown away when I first read Elena Ferrante because her writing was so intimate. One almost feels accosted by the proximity of her prose. But it was David Sedaris who got me talking about* The Candor Aesthetic. *I was driving around in hot Arizona in the summer of 2017, listening to him narrate his own diary,* Theft by Finding: Diaries (1977–2002), *on audio. I was not a new fan, but it was with this book that my mouth dropped open because of his unrelenting observation skills, his oft-unflattering depiction of himself, and his blend of humor and tragedy. Man, could he make himself look lousy to write well! I wanted to do that! Thus, The Candor Aesthetic was born!*

What I loved were the sharp observations, the absurdity, the self-exposure. Of course he published them, so everyone could see. DON'T EVER FORGET THIS: Writers gotta be read. Why bother if no one's watching? It's not solely a compulsion to write it down; it's also dependent on a relationship with readers. There must be an audience.

I suppose it can sound a little psycho. Why not keep internal meanderings to oneself? Why must one share?

There has to be some underlying purpose, right? A pursuit of Truth, Beauty, Goodness? An artistic vision?

So—shortly thereafter—I launched my own project, dubbing them my Facebook Diaries. *I posted them—to select friends. I just chose my audience the way I felt like it, frankly. My close friends (I left out a few, to be honest). A few writers (but not many). Some people who I just liked. Churchy types who could see through my bad language to my ecclesiastic soul-palpitations. People who could deal with my crazy politics. Folks who liked pets and streaming TV and hearted photos of my kids eating food. My mom, because, well, you know it wouldn't be cool to leave her out.*

Below, in tribute to Sedaris, are select entries. They're MOSTLY unedited.

Thank you, David.

You kinda blew me off unintentionally at your reading at the Orpheum in Phoenix (November 2017)—when I was getting my book signed, I wanted you to look deep into my soul and know me for the writer I am, and you didn't. I get that's asking for a lot.

An Ode to David Sedaris: When A Non-Famous Person Does What You Do (2017–23)

—this is for David Sedaris, and I don't care what anyone says

David Sedaris and I moved to New York around the same time, and we sometimes moved in similar circles. He was in Greenwich Village. I was in Greenwich Village. He did a show at La Mama. My friend worked at La Mama. He read at the Nuyorican Poets' Cafe, and I went to someone else's reading at the Nuyorican Poets' Cafe. He became David Sedaris. and I became Jennifer Spiegel.

Oct. 13, 2017

You remember that doc—a few months ago—who told me to stop shaving my armpits with a razor since I'm prone to infection?

So, I started waxing.

It's a $22/month thingy—not insane, a luxury, seriously so much better-looking than the razor—but I'm thinking I might cut it and keep Hulu, right?

So my saga. I'm one of those people who gets in the chair of the hairdresser or nail person or waxing specialist, and would prefer to just shut up.

If they must talk, I will get them to talk about themselves.

Madame Wax: 50-plus, all Ivana'd out—big hair, makeup, lives with an alcoholic and his mooching son who's in his late twenties, MAINTAINS A SECRET HOUSE with all her good things in it, runs a business with her ex-husband who sounds shady, always talking BIG money/lawyers/loans/ et al—like I get the impression she's rich.

But the funny thing. She'll be telling me a story and she'll say, "Well, like I told you last time, blah-blah-blah."

And: "Well, remember how I mentioned . . . ?"

At first, I would try to remember last time. I'd struggle mentally, pits exposed, hot wax buttering my body.

She told me about this? Did I hear this? I knew about that heist?

It took me a while to realize: She did not tell me anything before. Ever. It's her own narrative thread, left off, picked up, with whomever.

But who can keep track? The alcoholic doesn't realize she's got a secret house. And they've been together for seven years. And her ex owes her $15K.

"Remember when I told you last time . . . ?" she says.

And I'm, like, "Yeah, yeah. Then what happened?"

Oct. 18, 2017

Another tough night! We're just not sure that Melody doesn't have the whooping cough—she hacked for six hours straight last night, from 5 to 11 p.m. This, after our ER visit on Monday, at which they did test her for the whoop (results take two to three days!), but they also kinda blew us off and prescribed honey.

So, at 10:15 p.m., completely panicked by now, Tim and I decided to go back to the ER. We knocked on the bookshelf that my mom lives behind—seriously, there's an old lady who lives behind our bookshelf. Told her we were going and she should watch Wendy.

My mom talked us out of going—said it's just a bad cough, give her tea.

Back in our bedroom, after abandoning our plan, Tim says, "Am I mistaken, or was that the first time your mom talked some sense into us?"

Oct. 21, 2017

In Sedaris's book, he explicitly says how he thinks he accidentally hurt his dad with one of his books.

Oct. 27, 2017

Realized this morning that I haven't been to the dry cleaners in over thirteen years.

Nov. 6, 2017

Tim and I had this little heated thing this weekend. A fight. Yes, a fight. We've gotten better at it over the years, learning to move on. This time, we picked up ANOTHER COUPLE'S ARGUMENT. Like, I told him, and then he took up the guy's position and I took up the woman's.

Which is funny, but *not*.
Because, well, you know why.
We escalated.
It got ugly.
Simmering, boiling, explosive.

And then we calmed down (though Tim refers to me as "Jennifer Spiegel" and not "Jennifer Bell" when he's mad).

Then, we sat on the couch, spent from our dismal outpouring, having ceased in a faux truce. And I said, "So they'll get a divorce, and we'll still be married."

The end.

Nov. 19, 2017

Yesterday, Tim and I clashed in the morning over the girls' display of sheer laziness. It didn't escalate too much, but Tim said afterwards, "I had to go study a flowchart to calm down." #thingsscientistssay

Nov. 21, 2017

I've been thinking quite a bit about this, about my writing publicly, about oversharing.

I read this essay by Emily Nussbaum, which was really excellent, on oversharing and social media. Look it up.

Here comes some elitism.
I'm a freakin' writer.
A manipulator.
A performer.
That's right.

All artists are. And if you want the real elitism, it's here in my claim to be an Artist!

(DON'T DO WHAT I DO HERE. I AM A PROFESSIONAL. YOU ARE NOT.)

I can write a wild sentence with grammatical flourish, and a measure of philosophical gravity. That's my thing.

But you. Do not wax and wane or muse on existential conundrums here, on Facebook. Do not reveal marital woes or transform your spouse into your straight man. Do not uncover your nakedness, your foibles, your darkest moments . . . .

Writing is serious business, even when it's funny. And I think Nussbaum and others are right about the narcissism, the callow belief in ourselves.

Is there not value in the private moment? (Is nothing sacred?)

Must it be shared in order for it to be worth living?

I've just been thinking about this a lot, and I guess I'll say this:

The pen is mightier than the sword. You wouldn't play with bombs, would you?

Nov. 30, 2017

Melody gave *Sounder* one star on Goodreads, because the dog dies.

Dec. 6, 2017

This is a real conversation with my mom:

Mom: "Some guy tried to pick me up." She had just returned from Safeway.

Me: "Oh, yeah? Who? Was it the same guy as last time?"

Mom: "No. That guy is nice. He gives me chicken breasts."

Me: "Who was this?"

Mom: "I don't know. He was dressed nicely. But he said, 'I even have a Santa Suit.'"

It's the *even* part that gets me.

Dec. 11, 2017

Wendy said to me yesterday, "One of the things I don't like most about you as mother is that you haven't read Harry Potter."

Dec. 11, 2017

Apparently, the Scotch tape that Tim was looking for had gone missing, but really the girls had it the whole time. He was all, like, "Where'd you get this?"

They told him and he demanded it back.

They said they needed it.

Tim demanded it returned and said, "Do you want Christmas presents?"

Jan. 4, 2018

When I went to bed, Melody was still up (reading Harry Potter!). I poked my head in. She wouldn't look at me. I said, "I love you."

Then, she said, "Love you, too."

I closed her door, checked on sleeping Wendy, closed her door, and out comes Melody to hug me and kiss me and say, "I love you so much."

Feb. 28, 2018

Snickers (dog) broke his leg about a year ago, and a pin was put in. The pin is sticking out—and, understandably, it's bugging him.

So he had an X-ray, and the pin will be removed surgically next week. (I don't even want to discuss $$.)

But they drug dogs to do X-rays. He's still messed up. Awake and sweet, but poor boy—still loony-tunes. Hungry.

But the real story here: He pooped in the back of my car on the way home from the vet.

So, seriously, you've gotta imagine me, gray roots beaming off the top of my head, getting the big and sedated dog into the house, cleaning up crap in the Honda, and then doing the mom thing.

I think the best part, though, was later as he was recovering when we were all looking out the window for Snickers' pooping routine, and there I was, watching the dog squatting obscenely in the backyard, WHILE I ATE A HANDFUL OF PEANUTS.

March 6, 2018

I expressed some annoyance that U2 is going to all these places, like Omaha, but still not Phoenix, and Tim was all, like, "Would you give it up already? You did it. It's done. It's not even fun. You think you're having fun, but you're not."

March 6, 2018

Every time I go to my vet's office, I'm nutty. Like I'm the weird lady there. Not sure why. I say silly things. I can't control my dog. I just had brain surgery. My hair is cra-cra. Like *every time.*

March 22, 2018

I saw my brain surgeon yesterday—just to check out my incision. All is okay.

So I gave him my little spiel on how I'm a statistical anomaly, obviously doomed, a real disaster artist (forget James Franco), and that my head feels "weird."

He said, "Well, it's just your new normal."

Then, I said, "Isn't it crazy that I can't even pronounce your last name, and you apparently saved my life?"

April 1, 2018

Wendy went to a hockey game last night, becoming the first in the family to ever attend a hockey game.

April 3, 2018

Here's the progression of my early-adult onset of introversion:
    I don't know. I may have plans.
    I have kids, no.
    I have kids, no
    I have kids, thank God, no.
    I have kids, thank God, no.

No.
No.
I said no.

May 22, 2018

Yesterday, Melody noticed that I give the cats purified water and the dog regular tap water. She was incensed!
"Why?" she asked.
"Because I love them more," I said.
"You're a pig-eater and a Snicky-hater!"
Melody doesn't eat pig unless it's barbecued ribs.

July 4, 2018, Chicago

After the boat tour, which Tim said he "fucking loved," he said Chicago might be his new favorite city. Because, like a massive dork, he's all into industry, trains, weird stuff like that. Now, NOW, he's interested in listening to my audiobook of Upton Sinclair's *The Jungle* (narrated by Casey Affleck) about Lithuanian immigrants and the meatpacking district. Never mind that I recommended this last year. Never mind that.

Oct. 12, 2018

Poor Melania. The most bullied person in the world. All we ask of her is this—not "Be Best." Just be real. Admit it. You fucked up. You married for money. You're gorgeous. He offered you America and all the riches in the world. You had a kid. You love your kid. You're stuck and you're not super bright but you're still very pretty.

July 22, 2019

Today is the seventeenth "anniversary," if you will, of my father's death. Though my mom kinda wants the credit, I bet he got me into the writing thing by FORCING me to read *The Catcher in the Rye*. Couldn't pass up a puppy or a kitten. Taught me about Richie Havens and George Winston and Traffic. Mel Brooks, Gene Wilder.

He was the man who tamed my wild-hearted mom.

I know we will meet again. And though my mom is a little nutty and she's got this elaborate theory on pets in heaven, I will assert my belief that my dad is taking care of Bosco and Juju and Sunshine and Chessy and all the rest of them like some kind of celestial Grizzly Adams.

Rest in Peace, dad!

Rock on, mom. Don't hold back or anything . . . .

Sept. 3, 2019

Sometimes, don't you find yourself, like, clicking an article on, say, Justin Bieber and, then, you catch yourself and you're, like, *Why am I reading an article on Justin Bieber?*

June 30, 2020

Sacha Baron Cohen. What a crazy dude! Let's have coffee!

July 3, 2020

Hugh Downs died. This is 2020, indeed.

Aug. 2, 2020

See Trump's insistence on saying "China virus"? Never dismiss this, ever. His willingness to push forward with a terminology, no matter if it's offensive. Equivalent to calling a Black man "boy," if you ask me. Shameful and easy to excuse by fans but deeply horrible.

Aug. 31, 2020

I love Spike Lee, so there's that.
>In your face.
>He's got an agenda.
>Propaganda is artless.
>Just an agenda.

Spike takes his agenda and renders it aesthetically, so that he's simply awesome.

Dec. 8, 2020

In the middle of the night, I woke up. Story [Cat #1] was snoozing by me. I saw Beesly [Cat #2] sitting upright, just out of reach. I thought to myself, "There's a mirage of good things." I was so thrilled with my word choice that I almost turned on the light to write it down. *Mirage of good things!* BRILLIANT! Like a Shakespearean sonnet. Thankfully, I didn't get up and I fell back asleep.

I woke up and told Tim how I thought I was such a scribe in the moonlight with the cats on the bed.

The moral of the story: Go back to bed.

Jan. 8, 2021

Did I ever say I hate Trump? (Someone said I said that.) No, of course not. I know this because I really don't use that kind of verbiage except in the case of water chestnuts. I hate water chestnuts.

March 14, 2021

Melody and her friend—one of my faves because she's pretty goofy—were making a "movie" of *The Hunger Games*. Their names were Friction and Ricotta. I LOVE THAT.

March 23, 2021

My newlywed—*very* newlywed—*young* friend sent me a photo of herself wearing her *very* new husband's shirt. She wrote, "I'm wearing his shirt because I'm cold."

I told Tim because it's cute, and he was, like, "She's that blissed out?"

I mean, she's at the stage in which wearing his shirt is so amazing.

And I'm, like, "Remember when I wore your old Elmo boxers you never liked for six years straight till they were practically shredded from the washer and my fat ass hung out?"

March 27, 2021

Beverly Cleary.
 Now, here was a gem.
 104!
 Died in Carmel, California!
 Married for sixty-four years!
 I think I've read sixteen of her books, and I loved every second of reading them.

June 19, 2021

I have to let you know that I've watched "Hoarders" more than once, which is essentially letting you know I have a torture-porn problem.

July 5, 2021 (Summer Vacation)

 I'm in the hotel room in the White Mountains [New Hampshire] with Tim's family. Do I even have children?
 Today, Tim and I freakin' paddle-boated around the lake like some kind of middle-aged couple.
 Today, Wendy said that none of the teenagers want to sit with the adults at dinner because all we talk about is taxes and paperwork.

July 22, 2021

Wendy is watching the neighbors' cat, and they're the nicest young couple. Wendy has pointed out how their house is all Millennial. It's the sayings on the wall:
 "COFFEE."
 "BE THANKFUL ALWAYS."
 "IN THIS HOUSE, WE LOVE UNCONDITIONALLY."
 "BEST DAD."
 In a Gen X house, you'd see this: "FUCK THIS SHIT."

Sept. 19, 2021

Literal text conversation between Tim and my mom, over Snickers' diarrhea....

Tim (hypochondriac): "It's either that he ate an acorn or it's Stage 4 colon cancer."

My mom (Jewish grandmother, even to the dog): "I'll make him some boiled chicken."

Oct. 3, 2021

More dog stuff.

So, we were at the park, walking Snickers. All four of us. Yesterday morning. A bunch of little kids see us and want to touch Snickers. They do. Snickers is always good.

One little girl says, "We had a dog named Snickers...."
Other little girl says, "But he's dead now."
Back to the original little girl: "Yeah, he died in the fire."
My whole family says, "Oh, no!"
Other little girl explains, "Her dad left the oven on."
The original little girl adds, "There were ten dogs, and seven died in the fire. Three lived."
All of the kids are happily petting Snickers, smiling away.
The original little girl adds, "Yeah, our Snickers died in the fire."
We say, "Oh, no!"
Okay, we'll be going now....
C'mon, Snickers.

Oct. 28, 2021

One of my students said her mom gets their cage-free, humane eggs from Whole Foods, because the chickens' bios are on the carton.

Nov. 1, 2021

Here is a sign of my coming senility:

I forgot my old neighbor's name, even though I once went on a date with him. I didn't know it was a date till after, and then I was, like, *Oh, that was a date.*

Here's a sign of me aging:

Yesterday, at Fry's, I openly guffawed and made a *phew* sound when we walked past a stinky smoker, and Tim noted that I've lost my filter, like an old person. Unfiltered.

Dec. 1, 2021

In *Tiger King*, Carole Baskins kept an online video journal—like my Facebook Diary. I was embarrassed watching. Tim was, like, "Who does that?"

I was, like, "Well, I do . . . ."

Carole Baskins and Jennifer Spiegel! United in cats and public diaries!

Then she shared how, the other night, her husband had diarrhea, and I thought, "Would I do that?"

Why, yes. Yes, I would.

Dec. 3, 2021

FOX allows Fauci to be compared to a Nazi. No repercussions.

CNN gets rid of Cuomo for being involved in his brother's life.

Dec. 11, 2021

Do you ever just sit and think about how people from your past are not present in your life at all—and while you certainly may not give a crap about them, they ALSO do not give a crap about you?

I had one of those moments the other day—but I do sit around and think, "I wonder what X is thinking/doing, etc."

It seriously is my nature. I do this. I really do.

I wonder about the siblings of my kindergarten best friend who might've killed herself. What happened to Jan, Tom, and Danny?

I wonder what happened to that girl who supposedly had an abortion in our dorm. We weren't friends. As a matter of fact, we were indifferent to each other. But this secret made the rounds. Where is she now?

I wonder what happened to my beautiful Canadian roommate at NYU. Did she return to Nova Scotia? And what about the Bostonian hot Armenian girl who did Bowery and East Village avant-garde theater who used to hang with us?

I just do this.

But I get sad when I think about how it isn't mutual . . . .

Depressing.

I never know what I'm going to say in these diaries.

Dec. 13, 2021

Season Finale of *Succession*. At one point, Tim looked over at me slouched weirdly on the couch and asked, "Are you alright?"

I answered, "Yeah, I'm just marveling at the writing."

Kendall. Man, Oh Man.

Dec. 18, 2021

The other day I said to Wendy, "Will you please make me a cup of tea and bring it to me?"

Living with teenagers means she responded, "Why?"

I said, "Because I'm cold, and I have cancer."

It did not work.

Dec. 22, 2021

Snickers came home exhausted from the groomers—as if he'd been at the gulag.

Dec. 30, 2021 (Massachusetts)

Cousin Skylar's bunny, Nutmeg, ate Wendy's phone charger.

I just like writing that.

Tim said one of the most Dad things ever when the girls were telling us how they stayed up all night and made crank calls. He said, "Which is basically how people get killed."

We all stopped. Pondered.

Jan. 18, 2022

The thing about Cracker Barrel is—you know this is true—you always get a little excited and think it's going to be good, but it never is.

Feb. 21, 2022

I feel like I've been watching *The Walking Dead* my whole life.

March 26, 2022

The other day we were filling out medical paperwork for our millions of doctor appointments, and we had to disclose whether or not we have . . . IRRITABLE BOWLS.

I'm cooking up some sad essay titles:
Memory Farce
I Will Scar You for Life
We cannot possibly stop watching *Curb Your Enthusiasm*.

March 29, 2022

Those Ukrainians truly are bad asses.

Melody told me yesterday that I look like the most average woman ever.

April 16, 2022

I saw an ENT yesterday.

I either have allergies or a brain tumor.

No, really.

I try to prep Tim for my early demise, but he doesn't like that.

But I went to the ENT yesterday. I didn't like him. And he didn't like me.

Hey, guy, you try getting a brain injury, cancer, and brain surgery while having a successful marriage to a problem child, while your nutty mother lives in the backyard, and you have two angst-ridden teenage drama queens who are perpetually in need of all your money that you earned during the era of Trumpian anti-intellectualism—try it, buddy. THEN, YOU LOOK AT ME LIKE YOU'RE LOOKING AT ME WHEN I TELL YOU I THINK I'M DYING.

I get more like Larry David every day.

April 25, 2022

Yesterday, on Seventh Street, we saw a van with this painted on its back window: SAVE THE BLACKS. EUTHANIZE FAUCHI.

Tim had to hold me back from shouting out my window, HEY, REDNECKS! IT'S SPELLED F-A-U-C-I! But we were coming home from church, so he was probably right.

June 15, 2022

More on Snickers.

So Snickers ran into the backyard and appeared to be chomping on something close to the back fence, and he wouldn't listen to me when I called him. The other day, there were a bunch of teeny-tiny peeping baby birds out there.

Tim got him inside.

Tim yelled at Snickers, "I don't agree with that at all!!"

June 19, 2022

Tim couldn't remember the name of the disembodied voice we call "Alexa," and he was looking for some movie.

He says to me, innocently but seriously, "What's her name?" He looks at the TV, head cocked. "Lady Google?"

June 29, 2022

Wendy's job as a barista is great!

The other day, a guy tried to shoplift. He attempted to stick a coffee grinder down his pants. It didn't work. So, he put it back on the shelf.

Wendy and her co-baristas had to call security. Security had to remove the product and sterilize the shelf and surrounding area—like in a hazmat situation.

July 2, 2022

Melody, in the car, when Elton John came on Spotify: "He only had this ONE song."
    I slammed my foot on the brakes.

July 3, 2022

Melody, in the car, when Led Zeppelin came on Spotify: "They're so BASIC."
    I slammed my foot on the brakes.

July 19, 2022

Wendy had an interesting conversation with a homeless dude at work. He was talking a lot about *Donald*. She couldn't tell if he was talking about *Donald Duck* or *Donald Trump*.

July 29, 2022

We have returned from our family trip!
    We came home with Covid!
    First, Manhattan.
    I remembered *again* that I'm not really a New Yorker. I'm a fraud. Though I breathe easier in the West Village, and I can sit happily with my lavender latte and Italian cheesecake in Caffe Reggio, I know I don't really fit in with West Village chic—I can never fully give myself over to the hustle, the ability to sidestep the crazies. I am a girl who writes about Moral Absolutes and Christianity and politics, with a hint of Holden and Patti Smith, a touch of highfalutin get-me-to-the-Met combined with wannabe Ferrante tendencies. The social landscape of my beloved city is *demanding*. I'm too reclusive, too introverted, too much of a mom, and it spells sorrow for me.

But I do also tacitly resent the pretension of the non-NY world—the pretense of normalcy, the implicit self-righteousness of elsewhere.

I feel inclined to defend New York and its loonies, to defend its madness, to let everyone know that I felt safe the whole time; it was fine; they're all really just like us except more colorful and with strong accents. Man, I can't fully embrace life *outside* of NY either. All those pursed lips and pinched faces.

Must I be homeless then? Must I always miss it the moment I leave?

And then we went to Massachusetts. Tim and I will move there when we are empty-nesters. We will take our pets, my elderly mom, and my books. We will buy a foam mattress and a small New England house. We will carry on with our exhausting/exhilarating/codependent/bookish/impoverished foodie/scholarly/TV-loving/pet-entrenched/hot-flashing/puritanical/BLM/vaxxed/religious lives in a home with enchanted forests nearby for walking and restaurants that serve lobster rolls, and where my kids can gather round.

We also went to the beach. I did get to wear my *Wicked* T-shirt and finish my Dave Eggers book.

Oct. 15, 2022

You know you're in trouble when you can't wait to sit on the couch with your husband of five million years, watching "Dahmer—Monster: The Jeffrey Dahmer Story" on Netflix to relax.

Oct. 24, 2022

We have five scarecrows in front of our house, set up for autumn.
We pull out of the driveway.
Wendy says, "Grandma is turned around."
Melody adds, "Ma's pants fell down."
Don't that say it all?

Feb. 5, 2023

Amy Krouse Rosenthal, *Encyclopedia of an Ordinary Life*:
"I always got the words *pedestrian* and *Presbyterian* confused. I didn't understand why Presbyterians always had the right of way."

March 31, 2023

Someone should write an excellent short story about Trump under house arrest in Trump Tower!!!!!! #ICantDoIt

April 20, 2023

When we drive alone in the car, Melody and I often listen to one of three things (and we drive A LOT): her playlists, my playlists, or U2.
    She said, "Your music is sorta sad."
    Which is why I listen to U2. Which is decidedly NOT sad.
    "I'm a sad person," I said.
    "No, you're not," she responded.
    Interesting.
    That she doesn't know.

April 24, 2023

Confession: I don't really remember anything about *The Matrix*.

June 9, 2023

I think everyone hates my hair. I am a Morrissey song.

June 19, 2023

I want this on my grave:
    This is how you use a semi-colon when discussing Dead Jennifer's favorite rock band; she loved Bono, Edge, Larry, and Adam. She'd prefer if you avoided semi-colons, unless you know how to use them well. She was fine with exclamation points because Lorrie Moore taught her about their beauty! Maybe that last sentence needs a comma; maybe, it doesn't.

July 9, 2023

I like Taylor Swift. I mean, not much. But she's okay.

July 18, 2023

Wendy said that watching someone my age or older doing something on the computer is worse than watching a toddler at her work stick his hand in the toilet to grab his own poop.

Aug. 11, 2023

Melody's fish died while she was at camp. Tim cares. Said something hilarious last night as the fish died slowly, pressed against a rock. He said, "See, he leans on the rock, *because he wants to be loved*, and he wants that pressure . . . ."

Then, he added, "I know animals."

I'm, like, *Will you get rid of it before Melody returns?*

Sept. 26, 2023

1. I was very surprised the other day when Wendy recognized the Smiths playing.
2. So I played them all day.
3. I want these two bumper stickers:

   SAY HI TO YOUR DOG
   IF YOU HONK AT ME, I'LL KILL MYSELF.
4. You know life ain't great when you're looking forward to being alone and grading.

Oct. 10, 2023

Not only did my kids not know what I was talking about when I called Story [cat] "Puff Daddy," but they also had no clue why I sometimes sing, "Choppin' Broccoli." What's this world coming to?

Dec. 1, 2023

This is Wendy's review of Shakespeare's *King Lear* on Goodreads:

"Honestly, it was pretty good after Act 2."

Dec. 14, 2023

My friend, Toni, saw a cute dog yesterday, and she commented, "That little dog looks like he was put together by a committee."

VI

A Christian Creative Writing Aesthetic

Well, I better say something.

A Christian Creative Writing Aesthetic

You know, it only occurred to me to write this *after* I finished editing everything.

In order to "whip this into shape" for publication, I had to pause my current book project, a novel, tentatively called *Trauma Mom*. It's fiction, not didactic, probably caustic, funny (I hope), foul-mouthed (at times), lyrical (?), and still brewing.

But I paused. For this.

My myopic, personal, eclectic pet-project.

This.

Which implicitly begs a question, doesn't it?

I mean, haven't you wondered?

Why in the world does *Kids Without Horses* have a Christian publisher?

At the risk of alienating some people, allow me to address this now.

* * *

I have very little memory of the event, but I delivered a paper called "A Christian Creative Writing Aesthetic" at an academic conference in Seattle in 2003. What a crack-up!

Not the paper, but me at an academic conference!

Like, me being all scholarly!

The funny part now is that I thought, literally last night (in September 2024, making final edits), I should probably write something about the role of faith, and I went looking for that old paper. I couldn't find it! Like, it was gone! And then, then, *then*, myopic/personal/eclectic Jennifer (accompanied by our hovering new kitten, Lobster) went down a thought-trajectory that went something like this: *It's gone. No more. Disappeared. Not real. I claim it on my CV. But it's a chunk of my life, and it's fallen away, like parts of the polar region or an iceberg. I'm melting! I'm melting! I'm melting! I can't*

A Christian Creative Writing Aesthetic

even prove that I'm an "Academic." I have no proof! A part of me, obsolete. My writing, no more. Poof!

And then I found it.

* * *

Along with other *scholarly* efforts I had apparently kept in a binder:

"The Postmodern Moment: What's a Gen X Teacher and Writer to Do," delivered at a C.S. Lewis Foundation conference in 2001! My kids be like: *Can you drop this Gen X thing already?*

"The Redemptive End: Only the Good Die Young," delivered at an Arizona State University conference on The Sacred and The Profane in 2002. Stay tuned for *redemptive end* stuff.

Then, "A Christian Creative Writing Aesthetic." Seattle 2003.

Amazingly, I would carve out a career on the periphery of academia, teaching always, definitely more preoccupied with my kids and my own writing the whole time. However, I've said it elsewhere and it's true: I'm writing on the border. I've always been on the border. That periphery!

Am I being melodramatic?

I mean, *a little*.

* * *

Briefly, a Christian Creative Writing Aesthetic?

I don't want to waste anyone's time. When I read Roger Rosenblatt's "I Am Writing Blindly" in *TIME Magazine* on Monday, November 6, 2000, who knew that guy would articulate a core belief for me?

Writing is a human compulsion, reflecting our existential need for meaning.

Ouch. Did I just write that?

(This is my take on his essay.)

If I personally could give up the idea that there is meaning in life, I'd give up writing. But I can't. And I find it—yes, I do—suspicious when writers believe that life is absurd, but they write nonetheless. Maybe not suspicious. Sad, tragic. It's an unhappy place to be. To want to say *something*, to be devoted to saying *something*—but to believe it's *worthless*.

Yikes.

For me, then, an important question to ask about my writing life is this: Why am I doing it?

Because there is meaning to be had.

That's the first thing to know about the Christian Creative Writing Aesthetic.

Affirmation of meaning.

* * *

Well, I'm after a few things in my writing.

Meaning, yes.

Universality, too.

I want to render the particulars of a story (like *Trauma Mom*, in the works) in such a way that it has universal relevancy?

Sounds noble.

It is!

What good is it to share my *myopic, personal, eclectic* idiosyncrasies if it doesn't somehow, in some way, at some point, touch or move or speak to all people regardless of race, religion, gender, nationality, etc., etc.?

Shouldn't Art resonate universally?

Shouldn't it ultimately hit upon *what it means to be human*?

Is that what I'm doing?

Is that what I want?

I'm sober-minded. All I can really say is that I try.

That's the second thing to know about the Christian Creative Writing Aesthetic.

Striving for universality through specificity.

* * *

In reviewing my old paper, I see some intriguing stuff. I'll be brave. Here it goes.

I equated creative writing with the Edenic mandate in Genesis. While cultural relativism is the dominating temperament of many (most?) writers and it's chic to deny Moral Absolutes, creative writing is like Adam naming the animals—like Adam seeing a cat and going, "Cat." Identifying what *is*, what really *is*, truthfully (objectively?). It is truly a *cat*, not a *cat* today and a *skibidi rizz* tomorrow. Writers are naming things truthfully—not relativistically, but creatively. We are truth-tellers. We are masters at it.

Or we want to be.

Like, cats are so *cat*. (Cat owners know this. They get *cat*.)

We just name the beasts, you know?

To write well about something is to understand its nature. There is responsibility here, profound responsibility. It is subtle, requiring nuances, the ability to sense grief, weigh joy, read between the lines. Fundamentally, writers are naming animals. Practitioners of truth. Seekers of understanding. I do take it rather seriously!

That's the third thing to know about the Christian Creative Writing Aesthetic.

Profound responsibility in understanding.

* * *

And we better be gentle.

Man, don't be mean.

That's the fourth thing to know about the Christian Creative Writing Aesthetic.

Handle these things gently.

* * *

But it comes down to this: the redemptive end.

Hold tight, naysayers.

Three questions come to my depraved mind: Must every story end in a conversion? Should I mention Christ's work on the cross every time my characters find themselves in a bind? And does this mean that cussing is out?

I dare to answer all three at once: No.

It's all about meaning.

By the redemptive end, I am not suggesting that narratives must end happily. What I crave in my fiction is meaning. There is a kind of satisfactory closure in this. A sigh. An understanding. A narrative doesn't amount to nonsense, Hemingway's *nada*.

Boom! That's it.

Kids Without Horses

My favorite film of all time to discuss is *Pulp Fiction*. It is blatantly redemptive. I'm going to start sounding a bit affected in a sec. Just for bit.

Let me get my glasses.

(As I've pondered this section, I've been thinking that I need a caveat-of-sorts. I've been talking about *Pulp Fiction* in this way for so long in so many creative writing classes that I genuinely don't know the origins of much of my analysis. I suspect it came from my old friend, Tod McCartney. I'm going to give him credit for the possible origins of the *Pulp Fiction* analysis.)

Pulp Fiction is moralistic and non-relativistic. It clearly distinguishes between good and evil. Its content makes its title ironic. There is no pulp fiction here. Ultimately, there is redemption.

To get into it quickly, evil is identified as evil; Butch (played by Bruce Willis) is not "required" to save his enemy's life. But he does. He does, because evil is a profound and terrible thing.

I'm serious, watch the film again.

And then, of course, Jules (played by Samuel L. Jackson) is the Sage throughout the film, thinking about cleanliness and forgiveness. The most obvious example of this is when Jules and Vincent (played by John Travolta) pontificate about cleanliness while they clean up their car after accidentally killing a guy in the backseat. They discuss forgiveness while scrubbing the car's interior, trying to wash away the blood (reminiscent of Pontius Pilate declaring his hands clean of the blood of Christ). Later, Jules spares the lives of two criminals, Pumpkin and Honey Bunny, during a thwarted robbery. Not only does he spare their lives, but he also gives them money (this is akin to Christ ransoming sinners by His work on the cross). This character played perfectly by Jackson impressed me so much that I had to name a cat after him (way before Lobster), and I will love Jules, my beautiful boy, forever and ever (and I'm a forever-fan of Samuel L. Jackson, too).

Finally, the motorcycle on which the two characters ride off into the sunset at the end of the film is named "Grace."

For all its offenses, *Pulp Fiction* is highly, even religiously, redemptive. A modern-day parable. (*Oh, those golden Gen X nineties!*)

I'm actually not looking to get as blatantly religious as that in my own work. *Pulp Fiction* references the Bible and everything. It's not my thing. I feel, frankly, that I write for a secular audience. I do. (I write for secular audiences deliberately, and others may not choose this.) What I'm wanting to do is, well, render true things artistically? Exercise a kind of fidelity to truth? I want to understand the nuances of resolution, the craving for closure, the beauty of the end.

That's the final thing to know about the Christian Creative Writing Aesthetic.

The redemptive end.

(Allow me to toss out a few names here: James McBride, David Eugene Edwards, Harrison Scott Key.)

And now everyone knows why I have a Christian publisher!

* * *

Not so fast.

I gotta admit, I've never once read a book labeled as "Christian fiction." I expect it would *hurt*. Physically. I can't; I won't.

I do not listen to any Christian music, unless one counts U2. (And David Eugene Edwards or Johnny Cash—does Bob Dylan still say he's a Christian?)

I think I saw Kirk Cameron's *Fireproof*, but I don't remember it, and I doubt I liked it!

I would say that 99 percent of my artist friends are not Christians, and there's a big reason for this: *They're better artists.*

Any real Christian Creative Writing Aesthetic must take aesthetics seriously. There must be no aesthetic compromise!

So I ask Christian artists, where's the passion, the blood and the sweat and the tears, the vomiting on the sidewalk late at night in a Big City, the exhilaration of dropping your kid off at college coupled with the tight compression of your heart, the fear you might die even though you believe in hope, the love of a spouse who has the power to give you tranquility in one instance and make your soul collapse the next? Why can't we laugh like freaks over dark humor? Why must we scoff when a "bad word" is said? Why must we fear unorthodoxy?

Aesthetics, aesthetics, aesthetics.

I love the punch of the F-word. I love the braininess of Dave Chappelle, Trevor Noah. I love drama, comedy, not-so-much fantasy or YA. But, surely, Christians: We can do better.

I'm writing *Trauma Mom* right now. I expect to be read by a mostly secular audience as per usual.

At any rate, I'll end this stuff and get back to my border life.

Afterword
Marriage Scenes

It's my fiftieth birthday, and it's raining outside—so our plans are thwarted.
    Me: "We can go to the Musical Instrument Museum!"
    Tim scowls.
    Tim perks up.
    I perk up.
    Tim: "Don't we have a coupon for meatballs at IKEA?"

Appendix

The Moon Thought Thy World an Angel

I'm including a piece of fiction in the Appendix for two reasons. First, it's a "lost" story, originally part of my very first book, The Freak Chronicles *(2012). As it should happen, it might be about the sacred with a splash of obsessiveness over America and non-America. Frankly, I've always liked this story, and it was a bad decision by me to pull it.* Freak *includes "The South Africa Stories." There are five South Africa stories in that book—all fiction, all inspired by my stay there in the post-Apartheid/early Mandela days. They are late-nineties stories, already tinged in historicity and a bit of sorrow. This one will either be lost forever or have its moment right now: The Sixth South Africa Story. A second reason, though: I guess I ended up writing ANOTHER BOOK ON WRITING. There's so much repetition in these pages, so much worrying over the same themes, so many exercises in "getting it right." I think this story reveals how things might come together in one place.*

"I can feel the size of your country," Robin says to Rian the night before the trip, rolling away from him, releasing the body she now knows well. She likes the feel of it by her side, larger than hers but compact. Slim, taut. A smooth back like a plane or map, a chest latticed with muscle and bone—rutted, odd textures like undiscovered territory, a flat stomach like a dip in a canyon, a valley above marigolds. Even now, turned away, she knows his body like one knows a country: its layout, its cultures, its peoples. "I could never feel it at home."

* * *

Kids Without Horses

She never felt the size of America, could never grasp its landscape. Perhaps she had been too much a part of her own terrain to see its textures, its lights and darks.

When Robin first touched ground in Cape Town, South Africa, six months earlier, Harper was the only person in the nation she knew. In the early nineties, Robin and Harper had gone to Northwestern together, sharing an apartment in Evanston and decorating it with an admixture of kitsch (Nagel, an Elvis oil painting), irony (Dennis Hopper, Martha Stewart), and memorabilia (*Laverne & Shirley*, Shaun Cassidy). After college, Robin had stayed in Chicago, but Harper had moved around—landing, eventually, in the *New* South Africa.

In the late nineties, at Ravel Cafe in a trendy part of Cape Town, Harper—still ironic, but no longer nostalgic—conspiratorially leaned over her portobello mushroom quiche and whispered to Robin, who had just arrived in the country, "Stay away from Afrikaner men. When you date, date the English."

Harper, now twenty-eight, worked for a South African grassroots organization that promoted health and hygiene in the townships. *Apartheid* over, Mandela in the presidency, townships still a mess, South Africa was a hotspot for expatriate do-gooders. On the cusp of turn-of-the-century Africa, Harper repeated to herself: "Go with the English."

Robin was making a mental list of things to do immediately: *Get job, find flat, open bank account, date English.*

Harper suspiciously eyed the Cape Town café people (mostly white) around them: divine drink-of-water bodies, sleek blonde ponytails over the nape of ivory necks, pants spray painted onto twiggy legs, buff men in black shirts. "They're the guys you'll have something in common with—not those redneck Afrikaners. Sure, you're compelled to say *Umph!* at the sight of their sunburnt faces and rock-hard bodies." Harper leaned toward Robin. "But then—." She lowered her chin and spoke into her chest. "Take a look at their clothes. Note the serious need for the Gap." Crossing her arms over her body, she sighed deeply. "Go with the English, Robin. Go with the English."

Robin was silent; then she sighed, too. "You've changed, Harper." Another sigh of resignation. "What happened? We wore Birkenstocks. We waved white flags and boycotted tennis shoes made by poor children in less developed countries—."

Harper cut her off. "Robin, you have to understand something about South Africa right now. About Cape Town."

Appendix

"What?" Robin lowered her croissant sandwich and wiped honey-mustard from her lips.

"We missed it, kiddo. *The revolution is over*. We wanted to fight the good fight? We wanted to take a stand against *Apartheid*? It's over."

Robin stared into her old college roommate's eyes. "But here we are." Robin opened up her palms. "*Here I am*. I'm late."

"Don't fret—Cape Town is *in*." Harper winked. "It's the late nineties in trendy, post-*Apartheid* South Africa. Camp. Chic. Africa with Evian."

"I could only afford to come *after* the revolution." Robin crumpled up her napkin.

Harper said each word emphatically. "You may have come to fight the good fight, but it's too damn bad." She poked a cherry tomato with her fork. "*Other* people fought it. The president of this goddamn country is Nelson Mandela, you peacenik. You arrived at the same time as the model crowd, and there's *nothing* you can do besides break open the sparkling water."

"Oh. My. God," Robin said. "I wanted peace, love, and understanding."

"Be honest, Robin: You came because you were *bored, unmarried*, and *the exchange rate was good*."

* * *

On the morning that Robin and Harper leave for their road trip to the Kalahari in the north of the country, Robin wakes early and puts yellow Post-its all over Rian while he sleeps. On the Post-its, she writes, *It only seems like I'm gone*. She sticks them on his pillow, on his sheets, even on his bare shoulders. He doesn't wake.

* * *

Robin lived with Harper in Camps Bay for the first three months after she arrived in South Africa. From Harper's rented terrace, one could see the Twelve Apostles taking rocky shape in the mountains nearby—each Apostle naturally carved in stone, presiding over the coast like a scholar or a vulture. The Atlantic and the beach were before these rocky saints. Camps Bay was excessive, opulent, sizzling—suntanned whites sauntered on golden shores, and luxury homes with high-tech alarm systems and signs that said *Baywatch Armed Response* lined winding switchbacks down the mountain and to the sea. To the north, along the scenic freeway made for movie stars and sports cars, downtown Cape Town eddied, spiraling into a network of segregated suburbs, shantytowns and enclaves, suspicious quarters white girls were supposed to avoid. Afrikaner, English, Colored (this was the disturbing moniker for those who were multiracial), Xhosa and Zulu demarcated the landscape, dividing up fertile and scarred dirt. Camps Bay was a wealthy white hamlet, and Robin and Harper, foreign white exports, were suddenly rich girls.

The country was still reeling, hiccupping from its history, gasping for breath.

One early April morning, two months into Robin's sub-Saharan tenure, she joined Harper in the backyard. Harper was wearing a terrycloth robe, sipping instant coffee, and sitting on a lawn chair in the wet grass before the Twelve Apostles. When Robin opened the sliding glass door and stood before Harper, Harper said, "It's another fucking day in paradise."

It was an indictment, an accusation.

Another fucking day in paradise.

"What are you doing out here?" Robin cautiously sat down by her friend, pulling her nightshirt over her knees.

"Coffee. School visit today—there's a production of *Puppets Against Apartheid.*"

Without making a sound, Robin mouthed the words *Puppets Against Apartheid.*

Harper turned her heavy eyelids towards Robin. "You still dating that Afrikaner?"

"Yeah." Robin had immediately met an Afrikaner at work; she was an admin assistant (B.A. in Political Science with a minor in African Studies) downtown, and he was an engineer—an Afrikaner engineer. Not an English engineer. Rian took her for Thai, told her that her favorite book was overrated, gave a speech on the future of a doomed democratic South Africa, and then kissed her passionately and without warning.

"So is he a liberal South African or what?" Harper quietly asked, turning towards the sea.

"I suppose that depends on how you define *liberal.*"

These were expatriate questions, things expats asked one another over drinks and open passports. The two main white groups were the English, generally considered more progressive, and the Afrikaners, originally of Dutch descent and associated with the old *Apartheid* regime.

Appendix

"How does he feel about Mandela?" Harper blew on the surface of her instant coffee.

Robin scrunched up her eyes. "Well, he doesn't want him *dead* or anything."

"So, he's a liberal South African," she said flatly. No conviction in her voice.

"I guess so." Robin suspected that Rian kept a gun in his house, but she didn't want to know for sure so she never asked. She wove her fingertips together and wrapped her hands around her head.

Harper got a faraway look in her eyes. "Did I ever tell you about the time I went to the Karoo with some whities from work?" Harper stared into the dawn, a rich blur of yellow sun and blue sea.

"No." Robin blinked and whispered. The sun had begun to warm the grass, drying the dew.

Harper's eyes were still faraway. "We hitchhiked, catching a ride with a man who had disturbingly beefy fingers—."

"You shouldn't hitchhike," Robin interjected. "Especially if you see beefy fingers—."

"The whities wanted to go to this annual music festival in the Karoo." Harper stared at some invisible point on the horizon. "It was, like, Afrikaner Lalapalooza."

In her head, Robin pictured a crowd of Afrikaner hippie-chicks and peace-loving, secretly very attractive boys who desperately needed a good shower and a big city haircut. She envisioned a sloppy mud pit; she heard reggae, funk, and grunge; she smelled sweet marijuana, pungent incense, and something swampy; she also felt extremely thirsty. "So you went to the festival?"

"Yeah. Miriam Makeba performed." Harper fixated on the ocean. "I had just arrived in the country, and I wanted to soak it all in—you know?—absorb South Africa in every way."

"What happened?" Robin asked, noticing that Harper was tearing up.

"A few members of the audience threw stones at Makeba and shouted *Go home, Kaffir.*" Harper turned to Robin then, and their eyes met. "That's what they said."

Robin sucked air in through flared nostrils.

"That's like stoning Billie Holiday in the States." Harper put her coffee cup on the ground.

Kids Without Horses

The two American women were very quiet. They could only hear the distant shore.

Harper continued speaking. "*Miriam Makeba.* Do you understand?" She shook her head. "Fucking Nazis."

They listened to the tide roll in. For ten minutes, they didn't speak.

Then Robin asked, "Why do you dislike Rian so much?"

Harper gave a perverse smile. "Robin." She stopped, and began again. "He's from a different world. He may not be vigilantly racist, but you better believe he would be among those telling Miriam Makeba to *Go home, Kaffir.* Don't kid yourself—."

"He's a man, not a global epidemic. He's an individual, not a plight—."

Harper shook her head. "I'm sorry, Robin. I'm sorry." She poured her coffee out onto the ground. "I don't think you get it." Harper stood up. "Rian is the right age for compulsory military service—under *Apartheid* he served in the army. Do you know where he was stationed? Have you ever asked him if he supported a racist regime? Have you?"

Robin rushed to speak: "He was on the Namibian border. He hated it. All the men got crabs from their sleeping bags—"

"Ask him what he did in the army besides get crabs," Harper interrupted her, adding with sarcasm, "*from his sleeping bag.*" She glared at Robin. "Ask him if used his gun. Ask him about rolling tanks into townships or killing kids or torturing young Black men. Ask him—"

"Rian never hurt anyone—." Robin looked into her coffee cup, which she squeezed between her knees.

"Ask him about living under *Apartheid*. Ask him if he cared about the Black majority. Ask him where he stood, Robin. *Just ask him.*"

And then Harper turned to go back inside,

When Robin finally got up from her chair, and when Harper finally left for *Puppets Against Apartheid*, Robin thought, *It's another fucking day in paradise.*

* * *

Harper picks Robin up in her ancient VW bug and they take off for the Kalahari Desert in search of the Kalahari lion. They drive from the lush and fertile Western Cape, through Citrusdal and Clanwilliam, to the Northern Cape Province, stopping for burgers at a Spurs Steak Ranch in Upington. Upon parking the car and pointing out how tidy and how white

Appendix

the town seems to be, Harper says, "This place reminds me of *The Stepford Wives*—something's *off*."

At dinner in Upington, Robin stares at Harper, her overeducated, office girl/wealthy swashbuckler/discontented cohort (almost her replica) on this African adventure. Harper does something intricate and purposeful with ketchup and mustard. She looks very busy, extraordinarily mindful of her condiments, and Robin recalls a conversation they recently had over gin, at Obz Café, which is in Observatory, the Berkeley-ish suburb near the University of Cape Town. Obz Café combined everything vogue with a splash of minimalism and stark, chic, and pale things. With smooth, cool gestures, Harper had nonchalantly said, "We'll go back to America when our breasts sag. Until then, let's hang."

In many ways, Robin now thinks while sitting in the Spurs at Upington, that's what they're doing: *hanging*.

"It's been years since I've actually seen *The Stepford Wives*," she says to Harper, rolling a fry through ketchup.

Harper makes spooky seventies' sound effects. "This place probably isn't real."

Robin says, "I don't think it is."

* * *

Robin eventually moved into a rundown house in Rondebosch, a southern suburb of Cape Town, with Rian—Afrikaans, male, carnivorous. There was always the possibility that Robin, a foreigner with a work visa, would return to her home in Chicago and resume her life in desktop publishing or some sort of nonprofit work. There was always the possibility that corrupt politics would force Rian to move to England or Holland or Australia, where he spoke the languages and he could still be an engineer. Rian and Robin never discussed moving to the States together. Careful about birth control, cautious around controversy, and evasive on love, they tried not to think about the tentative quality of their nearly exotic existence.

* * *

Harper and Robin decide to push on to the Molopo Lodge, which was situated just outside of the Kalahari Gemsbok National Park, one of South Africa's famous game parks and nature reserves. They stop talking

Kids Without Horses

when they leave Upington around six at night. They're in the middle of nowhere, and they're tired and silenced. This is Godforsaken Africa. There are no tribes, no flora, no fauna. Only flatland. A lunar landscape. There isn't even the comfort of a mountain interrupting the *nothingness*. No Twelve Apostles, no sea.

Harper disrupts the silence. "Thank God we live in the La Jolla section of Africa." She looks at Robin. "Can you imagine living in the middle of nowhere?"

Just then, like a biblical plague, the VW windshield is bombarded by a million black, juicy, buzzing objects. "Dear Lord," Harper says.

Robin stops eating her apple and turns the Simon and Garfunkel tape off. "What the hell?"

Harper continues driving, while the black things pound the window, exploding into liquid upon impact. Robin freezes, all action suspended, the apple in her hand. "They're bugs," Harper says. "Locusts?"

"You think?" Robin instinctively backs away from the window.

"The gods must be crazy," Harper says, spanning her hand flat against the glass, flat against the splotches.

"Surely, we're gonna die," Robin says.

"Confess your sins," Harper shouts.

Then, just as suddenly, the explosions stop; the kamikaze bugs disappear and leave the windshield smeared in alien ooze.

"Gross," Robin declares.

"It is finished," Harper replies. "That's what Christ once said."

Robin looks at the gas gauge. "We're on empty, Harper."

Harper looks at the dashboard. "Crap."

"How much do you think we have left?"

"I can't tell. We're about an hour away."

Robin breaks into a sweat. "This reminds me of *Road Warrior*. Of *Ishtar*."

"A pack of lions will devour us like ribs at a Chinese restaurant," Harper declares.

"A band of angry Colored men will kill us out of righteous indignation," Robin replies.

Both flinch with the ethnic epithet, using it anyways.

"Roving white farmers will rape us and leave us for dead because they'll assume we're militant whites since we're in a VW Bug," Harper adds.

"I think I hear vultures."

Appendix

"We're gonna die."

The list of potential travesties is as endless as the chalky horizon.

Harper lifts her foot off the accelerator, trying to coast. Hoping for comfort and distraction, they play Harper's Road Trip Tape, Volume 6: *The Wonder Years*, featuring the Stray Cats, Jody Watley, and Culture Club. When Cyndi Lauper belts out that girls just wanna have fun, the car crawls. It sputters. It jerks. In the distance, the Molopo Lodge appears.

"Pray," Harper says. "Pray hard."

After long, dark moments in the dead of night and the thick of nothing, the car lurches toward the Molopo Lodge on the outskirts of the Kalahari Gemsbok National Park in the north of South Africa. The VW Bug runs out of gas as they pull up.

"We made it," Robin sighs. "We're gonna live."

Harper jangles the car keys. "Did you pray?"

* * *

On weekends, Rian and Robin often had dinner at Harper's, eating on Camps Bay balconies overlooking the Atlantic with European expatriates, all of them pseudo-beatnik, wannabe-bohemian, well-educated, with money in the bank. Rian, Robin, and the expatriates ate roasted red vegetables that lost their color in fire and grilled fish on darkened terraces illuminated by thin, braided candlewicks while discussing the aftermath of *Apartheid* and the future of Nelson Mandela. While they spoke, the ocean rushed madly to the African shore and retreated in steady, sad rhythms.

Once, Robin stood in the kitchen with Harper while Rian and the expats drank wine from Western Cape vineyards on the terrace. The refrigerator magnets were miscellaneous words that could be placed in any order—a swamp of verbal chaos. Harper had made her own sentences:

Never Seduce an Alluring Cupcake, To Thine Own Appetite Be True

Steamy Boy, 'Tis Some Passion

Hate That Man With True Spirit, The Best Splendored Affair Conquered Your Tender Virtue

Predestined Flame, Won't You Bewitch Me?

The Moon Thought Thy World An Angel

"Huh," Robin said, hands on hips, eyes narrowed.

"Poetry edition," Harper explained. She snapped her fingers. "You gotta get rid of him, Robin. He's too much of a Dutchman for you."

Kids Without Horses

Robin stared at the magnets till they blurred. How romantic, how poetic. She repeated a magnetized lyric aloud, breathy, like a Hollywood starlet from the forties: *Hate That Man With True Spirit, The Best Splendored Affair Conquered Your Tender Virtue.*

Harper, looking at her, said, "Come on, Cleopatra. Let's join the jet set. I made strong coffee. They like that."

On the terrace, Robin floated above the dinner party till a woman from Nevada drew her attention: "South African townships are just like American Indian reservations."

Another person said, "South Africa isn't any different from America in the fifties."

"What are you talking *about*?" a South African woman protested. "History doesn't occur in a *vacuum*. It's not like we're on our own historical *trajectory*, immune to events in the rest of the *world*."

Vigilant, upwardly mobile, pro-ANC.

Talk about a party pooper!

A Dane brought up corporate culture, multinational mergers. "We were taken over by a German company," she said dryly. "Now, I'm taking a night class to learn German."

Robin watched Rian delicately maneuver through this minefield of grace and pretense: individuals sipping wine, baguettes rising to polite mouths, eyes lifted in sparkly conversation.

Someone said: "Well, that's what the Germans are known for—taking over businesses and killing the Jews." The speaker laughed at his own joke.

No one said a thing. There were no patriotic platitudes. No one rushed in to save the day. The South Africans were used to this, used to awkward party moments in Cape Town, South Africa a few years before the new millennium, a few years after *Apartheid*.

Harper quickly stood, scraping her chair noisily against the terrace floor, catching moon in her hair. It was her dinner party, and she made a stab at levity. Gathering dirty dishes and pouring coffee, she sang, "Guess what's for dessert." She didn't wait for an answer. "We're making sundaes." She rushed into the kitchen, searching for hot fudge and maraschino cherries.

Robin followed. "I'll help," she said.

In the kitchen, Harper grabbed Robin's hand. "Whatever happens," she whispered, "at least we have the poetry."

Appendix

* * *

Harper and Robin sit on a battered couch next to an old pit bull named Sniper while their Molopo Lodge room is being prepared. Tired, dirty, and sweaty—Sniper between them—their eyes glaze over and they breathe through open lips.

A man with gray hair, a safari hat, and red eyes approaches looking like a weathered Marlboro Cowboy. With a drink in his hand, he stumbles forward: suave, debonair, old. "You two Americans?" He has an Australian accent.

"We live here," Harper says, her voice droll.

The Australian man takes off his safari hat and holds it against his chest. "You're headed to the Kalahari Gemsbok?"

"Tomorrow." Robin eyes the safari hat, wanting one.

"I just got back from Kruger. I've been to every major game park in the entire country." He puts the hat back on his gray head.

"Have you seen anything good?" Harper looks skeptically at him—as if there were *nothing* he could *possibly* say of interest.

He motions toward a bald guy at the end of the bar. "That guy over there saw a pack of lions this morning." Their eyes trail after his finger to a bar with countless safari hats bobbing at eye level. The hat-wearers throw back bourbon, Scotch, vodka, and gin in glass tumblers. The tumblers and safari hats fill the room. The bar is long. Everything is beige: hats, walls, skin.

"Ladies, you're all set." The Molopo Lodge woman stands before the battered couch. She's more pink than beige.

Following the woman to their room, Robin mumbles to Harper, "You didn't have to tell him we live here. We're not the Ugly Americans."

"Speak for yourself." Harper walks ahead, yawning.

* * *

Rian's closest friend was an Afrikaner named Craig who lived in Constantia with his Swiss girlfriend. In contrast to the Camps Bay crowd, Craig and his girlfriend served elaborate Indian dishes, Malay-inspired *bobotie*, and thick slices of red meat barbecued on burning *braai* pits in the back. Meat-eaters, always. Over dinner, they would discuss the Velvet Underground, road trips to Botswana, and, often, their jobs. Frequently the conversation became intense, loud, decidedly male; sometimes the participants gave way to excitement and began speaking in Afrikaans, letting English-speakers flounder or smile graciously. Robin would say, "Watcha talking about?" Rian and Craig would never answer. They just switched back to English.

When Craig's Swiss girlfriend left the room this one time, Craig said something awful about her. "She's a bore, isn't she?" He leaned forward when Robin scowled. "The sex is good. I need a roommate. Give me a break."

"You're a pig," Robin whispered back.

"And you rape the language," he responded.

Then the Swiss girlfriend entered the room. "Dinner's ready!"

They sat down, but the girlfriend didn't even join them; she just rushed around, bringing food to the table. When they ran out of papadum, Craig sang out, "Oh, Miss Papadum!"

"You're being a bit rough on her, aren't you?" Rian said in Afrikaans. Robin understood, but pretended not to.

Craig whispered, "She *loves* it. *Trust me.*"

Robin folded her hands in her lap, hating life, hating men, hating herself.

Finally, the Swiss girl sat down. "In South Africa, my relationships are different," she said, passing a bowl around the table. "Chutney, anyone?"

"How are your relationships different?" Robin dipped a spoon into the chutney and flinched when Rian touched her under the table.

"Here, I can be a girl." She smiled serenely and fluttered her eyelids.

Robin dryly responded, "It's true, there are benefits to reap from chauvinism." She paused. "Rian *always* opens the door for me." She added, "Can't beat that."

The men grunted. "You've really got to do something with her," Craig said to Rian, gesturing his thumb in Robin's direction.

"In South Africa, I'm taken care of," the Swiss girl said.

Robin nodded. "In South Africa, men are *men*, and women are *women*. It's nice to know you can forsake a little of that new-world independence. *Machismo* is alive and well—."

"I never ask you to be *dependent*." Rian turned sharply toward Robin.

"Sometimes, we'll go to the beach and Rian acts like a happy dog—he'll head out into the waves and leave me in the car with a book. He'll just leave me."

Rian was indignant. "But, Robin, you like to read."

Appendix

Craig refilled their wine glasses. "Isn't there anything you can do about her?"

Robin stared at Rian. "What if I didn't? What if I really didn't like to read?"

"Why do you put up with this?" Craig laughed and put his arm around his Swiss girlfriend's shoulders; she leaned into him, looking like the whole thing was delicious.

"The sex is good," Robin said, bitterly. "That's why he puts up with it."

"Robin's just being difficult," Rian said. "She's crazy about me."

Robin touched Rian's hair. "That's right—I *do* love to read. Even in parked cars."

The moment the Swiss girl left the room, Craig muttered to Rian, "You need to throw this American against a hotplate or something—make her more obedient."

"A *hotplate*?" Robin stared at Craig.

Fun and games behind-the-scenes, unbeknownst to Craig's lover.

Afterward, when the Robin and Rian got in the car to go home, Rian burst out laughing.

Robin was upset. "She mistakes dating a South African with being treated like shit."

"She's happy," Rian shrugged, still laughing. "It's okay. She smiled all night."

"So what? A love affair is only as good as its end. When she finds out later he never loved her, the whole thing will be ruined."

"You think?" Rian pulled the car out of the Constantia neighborhood.

"That's how it works. The end is *everything*."

For the rest of the night, Robin worried about South African gender roles, love in the States, the way the end shapes the history. She began to think about beginnings, about endings.

She knew that the end really is everything.

* * *

Harper and Robin enter the game park at 7:30 a.m. Both women have been to game parks before—Kruger in Mpumalanga and Hluhluwe-Umfolozi in KwaZulu/Natal; they understand Safari Etiquette: how one shares the road, how one generously offers up binoculars, how frequently words are spoken and at what volume. Lions rip bloody deer flesh off white bones in the wild. You gotta be on the lookout. Rules are followed.

Five cars line up ahead. Harper pulls over and leans out the window toward an Afrikaner in the next car. "What's going on?"

"The springbok over there is giving birth—a once-in-a-lifetime opportunity," he explains.

Harper positions the car so they can watch. Exiting automobiles is prohibited.

The springbok lies on her side on the desert flatland punctuated by a few scratchy shrubs on the desolate landscape. Her fur is the color of mushrooms and her belly is white and swollen. Inside her body, something twists and distorts the grace of her form. The springbok strains quietly in birth pains.

For a long time, Robin and Harper watch. Minutes pass; no one speaks.

Then, in the late-morning sun—blinding and hot—the springbok gives birth. A baby, a fawn: soft body, spindly legs. A symphony of faces leans forward in cars.

The springbok stands next to her fawn. Almost immediately, the mother climbs onto her feet. She licks the baby and prods it with her black nose.

The springbok nuzzles the new fawn, beckoning her to rise and follow.

Harper grabs hold of the steering wheel, clenches her teeth, and whispers, "Get up."

Robin squints, confused. "What's happening?"

Harper keeps her eyes on the springbok. "It has to get up." Harper hunches over the wheel. "Otherwise, it'll die—she'll have to leave it."

All around them, people in cars stare at the scene. Mouths drop open.

The mother pokes the baby. The baby struggles to ascend, struggles to stand on wet legs. She climbs to her feet the way cartoon deer do in animated movies. One leg steady—almost two. The baby collapses. The effort has made her weak. The baby tries again. This time, she barely makes it off the ground before collapsing into a pile of newly-born body.

Harper's voice breaks. "I can't watch this."

The mother springbok is confused. This isn't how it's supposed to work. Together, they're supposed to run off into the sunset. Together, they're supposed to flee from lions. Together, they're supposed to sip from cool waters.

What's happening?

Appendix

The mother slowly begins to walk away. She stops. Her ears twitch. She returns to the weak baby on the ground, too tired to even try. She prods, but the fawn doesn't move.

"No," is all Harper says. Robin is quiet.

The mother leaves again, stops, hesitates. Her ears flutter in the wind. She returns to the fawn, *her* fawn, on the ground, and then she faces the endless Kalahari. Resigned, she departs, leaving the springbok for dead.

The end is everything.

Harper turns to Robin, stunned. "I don't know what to do."

The other car passengers are shaken. Some cry. Enclosed in separate cars, people weep.

"What should we do?" Harper asks again.

Robin thinks, *There is a dead deer in the desert.* "Let's go."

"It's going to die out there," Harper protests. "We've got to do something."

Robin rolls up her window. "Start the car."

Gradually, the other vehicles pull away.

Robin says it again: "Start the car."

* * *

Sometimes, Rian and Robin would talk in bed while the rain fell on their tinny roof in wet sheets. Sometimes, they would talk in the backyard, eating cheese sandwiches on paper plates. Sometimes, they would go to the beach and get a pizza afterwards, talking the whole time.

Once, in the car, Rian said to her, "If I were a Black man, I'd be an activist."

Robin had asked, "Why not be a white activist?"

"I don't need to. The country is already mine."

Robin, taken aback, had responded, "You *do* realize you should have been shot while you slept in your beds, don't you? You *do* realize that this was a peaceful revolution and you got *lucky*?"

Rian had laughed at her. "This was no *revolution*, Robin. We *gave* them the country."

Robin hadn't known what to say.

The day after, Robin secretly called Craig. "Where were you in the late eighties?"

"In Botswana near the Okavango Delta." He got excited. "It was *great*."

"Why weren't you in the army?" she asked. "How come you weren't in the army with Rian?"

"I ditched, left the country. Do I look like I can load a gun?"

* * *

Around lunchtime, having said almost nothing to each other, Harper pulls up to a restroom in the Wilds and they take turns leaving the VW for the toilet. It's a weird safari thing. One just vacates the car, uses the bathroom, and returns.

Harper goes, then Robin.

When Robin returns, Harper is asleep—face smashed against the window like one of the alien bugs from the night before, forehead pressed flat against glass, mouth open, hair glued to the sides of her head in sweat. "What the hell are you doing?" Robin yells, slamming the car door shut when she's inside. "Why are you sleeping in the middle of the day in the Kalahari?"

"I'm surprised you noticed," Harper snaps.

"What's that supposed to mean?" Robin snaps back.

"I fell asleep."

"Yeah, well. I could've been eaten by a lion in the toilet. Would you have noticed that?"

Harper says, "You get what you give."

Robin is stung and surprised. "*You get what you give?*" She hesitates. "*You get what you give?*" She's indignant, enflamed. "No, you *don't*. If that were the case, we'd both be dead." She turns red. "What's with you?"

We'd both be dead.

Harper flares like a brush fire. "I'm so sick of your self-absorption, your ability to forget your world. You've always got to be at the center of everything."

Robin recoils. "What is this? Where's this coming from?"

"You're only concerned about yourself. When all is said and done, it's about you. Forget the dying animal, forget the New South Africa, forget racism—forget it all."

Robin, stunned, gapes. "What's this about? Are you talking about that dead deer or something else? Are you talking about Rian? Is that it?" In the tight space of the car, Robin twists her body around, much like the fawn.

Appendix

"Not *Rian*." Harper rolls her eyes. "But, of course, that's what you'd think. You spend your whole college career going to candlelight vigils and signing peace petitions, and, then, then, the moment you hop off the plane, you overlook Black townships and you don't even remember who Desmond Tutu is. You jump into bed with an Afrikaner. You're like an American businessman whoring in Thailand." Harper is red-faced. Veins throb. Her fists are clenched.

Robin cowers. "How dare you? How dare you attack me?" Robin raises her voice. "And what about you? What about you and your white guilt? Isn't that why you're here? Look at you, fighting for human rights but unable to actually deal with *anyone* on a personal level. You like your problems to be imposing, widespread, and distant. God forbid, a real person shows up at your front door—."

"You're the one who sold out—." Harper spits when she speaks.

Robin ruptures like a volcano. "Don't talk to me about selling out. You see Rian in black and white; you see this country as a phenomenon. You have no *real* love of humanity—."

"For you, Robin, South Africa is a language immersion program, like moving to Guadalajara for the summer without speaking a word of Spanish—." Harper folds her arms across her chest and looks forward, staring through the windshield into the barren landscape.

Robin is silent. She measures her environs. Harper's face is hardened. In that instant, Robin knows her friendship with this woman is over. The attack was too vicious, too final.

A relationship is only as good as its end; this is the end.

She also knows her boyfriend doesn't love her and she doesn't love him. There was too much truth in Harper's assault. In the middle of nowhere, she is alone.

"Drive," she says. "Leave."

* * *

After Robin and Harper had settled into their own private lives in Cape Town, they often had to make time to see each other.

Only two weeks before the Kalahari, they went to the Cape of Good Hope. Winding along the shore where the sea hugged the land, they passed one fishing town after another till they arrived at the southern tip of the African continent.

Kids Without Horses

The landscape was as alien as the Kalahari, but different. Dr. Seussy bushes popped out of the earth in pretty green surprises. The Indian and Atlantic collided in oceanic argument. Baboon and springbok ran untamed over the panorama. White sand covered whole patches of earth—empty, romantic, frightening. There were touristy spots, but mostly it was African wilderness: shy deer or bold monkeys, plants from other worlds, a wild ocean.

There, at the Cape of Good Hope, the world reached a crescendo.

Robin and Harper, only a couple of weeks before the Kalahari, sat on rocks, looking out at where the two oceans violently smashed against each other.

"We're on the edge of the world," Robin said.

Their skirts were whipped by the wind; their hair flew like frightened geese.

Harper stared at the sea like a captain of a ship. At the tip of the New South Africa, she turned to Robin and reprimanded her: "It's just someone else's center."

Robin watched the crashing water, feeling rebuked and ashamed. It's just someone else's center. She remembered Harper's words: "Whatever happens, at least we have the poetry."

You Know That Song

As a great big pop culture-phile and a faux-academic, I'm torn between my sheer love of the "Fair Use" rule in referring to the *best songs ever* and the need to properly cite in MLA, like a good English prof. (I suddenly feel a wave of commiseration with my students: *But I don't want to format properly.*)

Below is a list of works (though other books, authors, and musicians are mentioned by name) within *Kids Without Horses* (footnotes are used, if it's not clearly referenced within the text):

Books

Jimmy Santiago Baca's *A Place to Stand*, 2002
Bono's *Surrender: 40 Songs, One Story*, 2022
Margaret Wise Brown's *Goodnight Moon*, 1947
Janet Burroway's *Writing Fiction: A Guide to Narrative Craft*, 2019
Rachel Held Evans' *Year of Biblical Womanhood: How a Liberated Woman Found Herself Sitting on Her Roof, Covering Her Head, and Calling Her Husband "Master,"* 2012
Elena Ferrante's Neapolitan Novels, 2012–15
Leslie Jamison's *The Empathy Exams: Essays*, 2014
Leslie Jamison's *Make It Scream, Make It Burn: Essays*, 2019
Amy Krouse Rosenthal's *Encyclopedia of an Ordinary Life: A Memoir*, 2005
Ann Patchett's *These Precious Days*, 2021
Marilynne Robinson's *Home*, 2008
David Sedaris's *Theft by Finding: Diaries (1977–2002)*, 2017
Rick Springfield's *Late, Late at Night*, 2011
John Steinbeck's *Travels With Charley: In Search of America*, 1962

Films

Quentin Tarantino's *Pulp Fiction*, 1994

Essays

Roger Rosenblatt's "I Am Writing Blindly" in *TIME Magazine*, Nov. 6, 2000
I mention having read something by Emily Nussbaum but I can't find it.

Songs

Duran Duran's "Rio"
Gin Blossoms' "Hey Jealousy"
Indigo Girls' "Closer to Fine"
Indigo Girls' "Prince of Darkness"
Led Zeppelin's "Babe I'm Gonna Leave You"
Alanis Morrisette's "You Oughta Know"
Buffalo Springfield's "For What It's Worth"
Bruce Springsteen's "Born to Run"
Cat Stevens' "Wild World"
U2's "Running to Stand Still"
The Verve's "Bittersweet Symphony"

Big Thank You

When I consider the book as a whole, I think of many friends. A very special shout-out to Ann Miller, Toni Muma, and Sandi Van Lieu—my kind of women. I probably wrote/revised/collected, like, 80% of this book in your presence—and *every single moment* with you guys is supreme. (We'll still do Park City when I move, right?) Thank you!

I thank my publishers, Wipf and Stock, for publishing me! It's a big deal to be embraced by this community. I'm a bit crazy, oft-displaced, eccentric, and this is where I want to be. Thank you!

Karen Craigo is the best copyeditor ever, and she's copyedited all of my books, except one! The first time was a happy accident, and I'm so grateful that you still let me call on you. Thank you!

Thank you to Ian Creeger for patiently and conscientiously enduring my endless typesetting tweaks. It's gotta be easier with other writers. I truly appreciate it!

And, of course, Kyle Minor who discovered me! Congrats on your new book!

That politics part needs some attention.

In writing my defunct political book, I read a lot—and some of those books and authors were especially influential on my thinking during that weird season.

This is the book that most informed my opinions: *The Spiritual Danger of Donald Trump: 30 Evangelical Christians on Justice, Truth, and Moral Integrity*, edited by Ronald J. Sider. (We share publishers!) I can safely say that it is the closest to my own convictions. (I'd love to read a follow-up from these same authors. Hint-hint!)

There were other big influences. Jaron Lanier (who was featured in the documentary, *The Social Dilemma*) wrote *Ten Arguments for Deleting Your Social Media Accounts Right Now*, and it pretty much got me thinking.

There are other sources talking about algorithms and the effects of this online community-building that requires no real intimacy—but Lanier was pivotal. (A very recent influence: Jonathan Haidt's very good *The Anxious Generation*.)

Valeria Luiselli wrote a masterpiece of a novel with *Lost Children Archive*. It influenced my politics!

Ta-Nehisi Coates, who isn't an MLK-phile like I most certainly am, wrote a favorite with *We Were Eight Years in Power: An American Tragedy*.

In the midst of the Trump Era, I was a live wire, easy to set off. I think, frankly, Spike Lee's very new New York stuff is the most hard-hitting of all the films and TV I saw during my obsession.

As for the other meanderings, I absolutely must must MUST give a great big *thank you* to the readers of my TOP SECRET *Facebook Diaries*. (Forget that deleting-your-social-media stuff!) Man, you're all so faithful, so affirming, so quick to be kind! And, trust me, I've re-read a lot of it—and there's a ton of embarrassing nonsense in there. Thank you, friends! Like, *really*.

I'm a cruel cynic, so when I say that Tim Bell is my soulmate, that's something. Thank you for fighting the good fight with me. I love you. I can only tell anyone who will listen that my daughters are my treasure, my life. I just love you both to pieces. I thank my family forever.

This is for my mom, that formidable, Carole-King-*Tapestry* powerhouse of a woman. As I used to write on every single homemade card in childhood: *I love you. You are love.*

www.ingramcontent.com/pod-product-compliance
Lightning Source LLC
Chambersburg PA
CBHW071201160426
43196CB00011B/2159